Wilhelmina's

WORLD OF

Child

Modeling

By
Natasha Esch
President, Wilhelmina Models

CAREER PRESS
180 Fifth Avenue
P.O. Box 34
Hawthorne, NJ 07507
1-800-CAREER-1
201-427-0229 (outside U.S.)
FAX: 201-427-2037

WILHELMINA'S WORLD OF CHILD MODELING

ISBN 1-56414-141-1, $14.95

Cover design by A Good Thing, Inc.

Printed in the U.S.A. by Book-mart Press

To order this title by mail, please include price as noted above, $2.50 handling per order, and $1.00 for each book ordered. Send to: Career Press, Inc., 180 Fifth Ave., P.O. Box 34, Hawthorne, NJ 07507

Or call toll-free 1-800-CAREER-1 (Canada: 201-427-0229) to order using VISA or MasterCard, or for further information on books from Career Press.

Library of Congress Cataloging-in-Publication Data

Esch, Natasha, 1971-
   Wilhelmina's world of child modeling / by Natasha Esch.
      p.   cm.
   Includes index.
   ISBN 1-56414-141-1 : $14.95
   1. Child models--United States--Vocational guidance. 2. Children in advertising--United States. I. Title
HD6247.M772U528   1994
659.1'52--dc20

94-29095
CIP

Contents

I would like to thank the following people for their support and unmatched help:

Alison N., Donna M., Ellen S., Fran P., Jade A., Jen G., Nancy W., Randall H., and all the Wilhelmina models, their families, and staff.

Special thanks to
Gordon Bass of Model Properties.

Introduction
The World of Child Modeling

Photo by Jade Albert

You can't help seeing child models every day. Beautiful bright babies, radiant rascals, mischievously smiling toddlers, gorgeous teens, beaming from the pages of magazines and catalogs, laughing and dancing across the television screen, and shining out from an incredible array of places including billboards, bus shelters, packages, and book covers—in fact, they appear in almost any place you can imagine. You can't help but take a second look at these kids who brighten our days and bring smiles to our faces. They capture our attention and make us notice a product or pick up a magazine, pay attention to an article, or help parents decide on back-to-school clothes for their kids. Some of them, like the Gerber baby, present warmly remembered images that we've grown up with, while other kids who appear are children that you have seen in a dozen magazines and advertisements without realizing it.

Did you know that there are thousands of kids working in the child modeling industry today? Some are only a few months old and still in diapers, while others are teens who are almost ready to graduate to adult modeling. Though different, they all have something in common: they are having fun, enjoying their time as young stars, and learning about success—and sometimes

Photo by Jade Albert

failure—and saving money for the future. Modeling has taught them to balance work, school, and family, and they all have a full and productive childhood. But who are these star kids and how did they get there? Is there a secret to their success? And most importantly, how can you get your child in the spotlight?

This book will familiarize you with the child modeling industry and tell you how you and your child can get involved, even if you don't know a thing about it now. It's a business that can bring tremendous rewards for parents and children alike, from the pride of appearing in the spotlight to the security of a paid college education or a substantial nest egg. Once you get started you'll discover that the modeling industry is filled with wonderful and talented people who have dedicated their careers to working with children and their families, and who are ready to help you along the way. Reading this book should be your first step. It will answer some questions you've been thinking about as well as those you haven't considered yet. And very importantly, this book will prevent you from wasting a single dollar on the multitude of shady operations that exist only to take your money, the "agencies" that charge for consultation and pictures, dazzle you with high hopes and promises of work, and then take your money,

Photo by Jade Albert

never to be heard from again. While in this industry I've heard too many stories about people who have learned about this the hard way. That's why I've written this book. I'm going to tell you the right way to approach the child modeling industry and have a prosperous career, so read on!

Chapter 1
Model Tales

Photo by Randall Harris

Let's take a look at a day in the life of a model in New York:

It's nine o'clock in the morning on a warm summer day in New York. Cathy Miller's alarm clock rings and wakes her and her seven-year-old daughter Chelsea out of the deep sleep that is the result of long days of hurrying from studio to studio in the madness of Manhattan.

Cathy's first act of the day is a telephone call to her daughter's modeling agency.

"Hi, it's Cathy Miller. Is there anything for my daughter Chelsea today?"

"Good morning, Cathy! Let's see, there's a go-see at two this afternoon that I want Chelsea to go to. Can you make it? Great! It's for a bicycle ad, so Chelsea should wear something casual. Shorts and a tee shirt will be fine. Let me give you the address."

Cathy carefully takes down the time and location of the studio.

"Thanks—and good luck!"

It's still early, and it's not too hot yet, so Cathy and Chelsea decide to spend some time in Central Park before the go-see. From their

apartment it's a 10-minute subway ride and a short walk over to a tranquil spot in the center of the city. Cathy spreads a blanket under a tree and thinks about the incredible trip from Oregon to the excitement of a modeling career in New York.

It was a year earlier that it all started. Cathy and her daughter were out shopping at the mall after school, looking for just the right dress for a friend's wedding. Chelsea was going to be a flower girl, and Cathy thought she looked absolutely like an angel in her dress as she tried to stand still for the fitting. She knew her daughter was both excited and nervous about the wedding.

As Cathy waited for Chelsea she became aware of a woman admiring her daughter with a smile. The woman approached Cathy.

"You have a beautiful daughter," she said. "Has she ever done any modeling?"

Cathy laughed. "She's something, isn't she? No, she's never modeled. I've never even thought about it, though she has been in some school plays and she loves being in front of people!"

Photo by Wilhelmina Models

The lady handed Cathy a business card. "My name is Lisa Masters, and I'm a modeling agent at Kid Biz Models. Why don't you give me a call? I'd like to talk to you." Lisa Masters turned to Chelsea. "Hi! What's your name?"

"I'm Chelsea, and I'm going to be in a wedding! Do you like my dress?"

"It's beautiful! How old are you, Chelsea?"

"I'm seven, but I'm going to be eight in September. I'm in the second grade now!"

The agent smiled at Chelsea and her mother. "Please give me a call. I hope to hear from you soon."

That evening Cathy spent a lot of time thinking about what had happened. Wasn't it too good to be true? Of course, she thought that Chelsea was beautiful, but could she really be a model? She'd heard about all of the scams in the modeling industry. Maybe it would be best not to call...but maybe Chelsea really did have something special. Anyway, she could investigate a little further. It couldn't hurt.

Photo by Wilhelmina Models

The next day Cathy called Lisa at Kid Biz and arranged a time to bring Chelsea in for an interview with Lisa.

Cathy and Chelsea arrived promptly at the agency and waited patiently to be seen. After a few nervous minutes Lisa entered and warmly welcomed them to the agency. "Please follow me," she said, and led them to a brightly decorated room full of toys.

Lisa asked Chelsea a lot of questions about school, about what she liked to do, and what she wanted to be when she grew up. To Lisa the answers weren't as important as the vivacity that Chelsea presented when she answered the questions. She was full of energy, curious, and, it seemed, ready to take on the world.

Lisa also discussed modeling with Cathy. "Do you work? Managing your child's career can be a full-time job if she becomes successful. How much time can you devote to running around town from assignment to assignment? These are things you have to consider."

Cathy finally agreed to a month-long trial period. She would let Kid Biz represent Chelsea for four weeks to determine how much work she might get and, more importantly, if they enjoyed the work and the new lifestyle that it would entail. This test period

9

Photo by Wilhelmina Models

would also give Kid Biz the opportunity to see how clients reacted to Chelsea. For the next month Cathy would call the agency each morning to find out if there were any go-sees, or auditions, for Chelsea to go on. At the end of the month Kid Biz could choose to offer Chelsea a contract.

The following four weeks went by in a blur. Chelsea got her first go-see the day after the interview, and the photographer that she met was thrilled to work with the new starlet. "She's a real natural," he said. He even called the agency to tell Lisa how much he enjoyed working with her.

Chelsea was on her way to success.

Unfortunately, things don't always go so well. As thousands of aspiring models discover every month, for every legitimate agency it seems that there are a dozen shady operations—and every time one goes out of business, another springs up in its place. This is what happened to another family:

In Dallas, John and Julie Jones saw an advertisement one day in the "help wanted" section of the paper. "Models Wanted! Any age, any type, needed for advertisements and commercials! Earn $1,000 a day and more!" The ad seemed to jump off the page at

them and fill their heads with visions of fame for their four-year-old son Jason. It was true that he was a great looking child; with his bright blue eyes and sandy blond hair he was truly an all-American boy. Why not, they thought, and called the number to get more information.

"Agency," answered a tired-sounding voice at the other end.

"Hi," began John. "I'm calling about the ad in the Sunday paper...."

"What time can you come in?"

"Well, I had a few questions first...."

"You'll have to make an appointment. What time? How about tomorrow afternoon at three?"

"Well...okay. What's the address?"

The next day the Joneses arrived at the agency. Only it didn't look exactly like what they thought an agency would. It was a small suite of rooms in a half-empty office building; there were a few pictures of child stars on the walls, but John and Julie were pretty sure that Macauley Culkin and the Olsen twins weren't represented by this agency.

Photo by Wilhelmina Models

A receptionist took their names and seated them in a waiting room full of impatient parents and their children. They noticed that the receptionist spent most of her time making appointments for people to bring their children in for interviews.

After half an hour they were called back into a small office in which there were only a couple of chairs and a desk. It seemed like the agency hadn't been in this location very long.

"You must be Eric!" said the agent, a large smiling man in an expensive suit.

"Um, no, I'm Jason."

"Sure, sure. How are you, Jason? And you must be his parents? Let me tell you right now, this child is a star. A kid like this hasn't come through my door in ages, and let me tell you, I've been in this business for a long time! Just look at those eyes! Yes, this kid is going places."

The Joneses couldn't help but be excited. A star!

"Let me ask you a question," said the agent. "If I told you that I could get a job for Jason today and he could make $500, would you say yes?"

Photo by Wilhelmina Models

The Joneses nodded.

"Great! That's the kind of attitude I like to see! Let me see Jason's composite."

The Joneses looked at each other. "Composite?"

"Jason will need professional pictures before he can get work. I need to send them to potential clients. So, you don't have any professional pictures, I take it? That's too bad. I'd like to put Jason to work as soon as possible. Wait, I have an idea. Here's the number for a great photographer. Give him a call and get a set of composite cards made. Then give me a call and we'll get started!"

The next day Julie Jones called the photographer. When he told her that a photo session and a set of 100 composite cards would be $500, Julie was shocked. But she was determined and, after all, the photos would pay for themselves in no time. She made an appointment for the next day.

The Joneses never knew that half of the money went back to the agency as a kickback.

Photos by Wilhelmina Models

A week later the pictures came in the mail. Armed with a new stack of composites, Julie called the agency again and asked for the agent that had interviewed Jason.

"He's not in the office at the moment," replied the receptionist. "Can I take a message?"

Julie left her number and the message that they had received the composites. But the agent didn't call back that day. Or the next. Julie called again and left another message. This time she was told that the agent was in Los Angeles for the week. Well, at least it sounded like he had business in Hollywood!

A week later Julie finally got the agent on the phone, but it was difficult to believe that it was the same man who had been so excited by Jason. He certainly didn't seem very enthusiastic.

"Send us 50 cards. But remember, there's no guarantee that we can find work. No agency can promise jobs. It's a tough business. I'll call you when something comes up."

But the calls never came. The Joneses were too embarrassed to tell anyone what had happened, since they were beginning to get the feeling that they had been conned. But they made a call to the

Photo by Wilhelmina Models

Better Business Bureau and learned the truth about their agency. It had only existed for six months, yet in that time there had been fifty complaints. It fit the standard profile of a scam—no legitimate agency would have required the composites. The Joneses realized that the only money made by the agency came in commissions paid by the photographer that they sent their aspiring models to.

The Joneses were angry and disappointed. But there was nothing they could do. They had learned a hard lesson about the industry.

Chapter 2
The Beginning

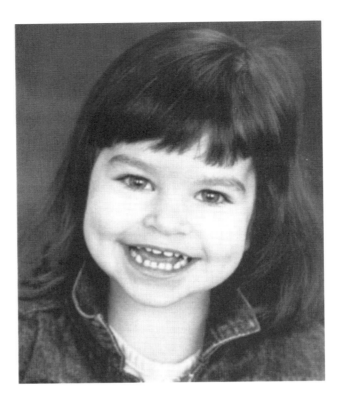

Photo by Wilhelmina Models

What does it take for a child to become a successful model? That's a tough question, because there are a lot of answers! Do you think that your child has the special spark that it takes to catch the attention of the public? Do strangers constantly turn to look and smile or stop you to remark upon your child's great looks and charm? Is your child naturally outgoing and eager to try new things and meet new people? These are some of the traits of successful child models. They're not only attractive, they're filled with the joy of life and seem ready to tackle the world. Shy? Child models don't know what it means! They thrive on seeing new people and places and trying new activities, and love the energy and excitement of their chosen professions.

And what about you? It takes a very special kind of parent to get involved in the hectic world of child modeling. Do you have the time and patience to manage a career? Is your child's happiness more important to you than the potential money and bright lights involved? I won't tell you that child modeling is always easy, and it's certainly not a "get rich quick" way to make money without work, but the end results are well worth the effort. Today thousands of children and their parents across the country are having a great time and earning money in an exciting and glamorous

Photo by Wilhelmina Models

industry. They are able to maintain a healthy balance of work, school, and play, getting the most out of life. Children are only children for a short time, though, and the modeling industry is always looking for new faces. Why not your child?

Before you read any further, ask yourself the most important question: Does my child want to model? Think honestly about his or her behavior and personality. Is your child comfortable around strangers? Does the child enjoy being the center of attention and the star of the show? Does your child have a spark that appeals not only to friends and relatives but everyone you meet? These personality traits are of the greatest importance. Before you send off those cute pictures, talk to your child about your plans. Not all kids are ready for the fast pace and excitement that are integral parts of the work. Some kids are naturally shy, while others may resent the time that they have to spend on interviews, go-sees, and shoots. They might rather be playing Little League baseball or practicing piano—and that is something that you must accept as a parent. Your decision to pursue modeling must be one that is fully supported by your child. You are going to be a team, and you can't work together unless you have the same goals.

I'm certainly not telling you to be a "stage parent." What are stage parents? Everyone in this business knows them—they're the ones that are more interested in modeling than their children are, the ones who push their kids into the business even when it's pretty clear that the kids don't want to be there. Unfortunately, there are parents who try to live their own dreams of fame and success through their children. Don't push your kids. Let them decide what they want to do.

You'll know your child has a desire to model if he or she is the type that immediately hams it up whenever a camera is present, or is eager to show off new toys to visitors, or perhaps even points to a child in a magazine or on television and says, "I want to do that!" Even if your child can't talk yet, his outgoing and animated behavior will show you whether he is eager to try the modeling industry. Now, how do you know if your child is the right type?

The Right Type

There will always be a demand for beautiful people and children in this business. Beauty sells. A child with crooked teeth or a large nose will probably get less work than a perfectly proportioned

child with a gleaming white smile and all-American features. Still, there is also a constant need for "real" looking kids with the imperfections that reflect a less-than-perfect audience.

If you ask an agent what she is looking for when she meets a child at an interview, you'll get an incredible array of answers. You will quickly discover that there is no "one" type that agencies are looking for. Child models must be marketable. What kinds of kids are marketable? ALL KIDS ARE! Unlike adult models who must conform to a very rigid set of measurements and characteristics, child models come in all shapes and sizes. At one time an agency will need a kid who has a perfect smile, while at another time they will need a child who is missing his front teeth. An agency may get a call for a short, overweight model and a tall, thin athletic type on the same day. What about a tap-dancing two-year-old or tiny ballerina? You would be surprised at the varied needs of clients!

The single most important trait for a child model is that of being photogenic. It's something that goes beyond simple beauty; while it may partly be determined by bone structure it's more of an over-all radiance that shows that the child loves being the center of attention and loves being photographed. He must be also be comfortable with the lights, camera, and activity on a set. Nobody, not

even someone who has been working in the business for years, can tell you exactly what makes a child photogenic. You really can't tell until you've seen a photograph or a finished advertisement that you can't take your eyes away from, one that makes you want to take a second look. You respond in a positive way. Some kids have rather ordinary looks but take great pictures, while others that are unquestionably beautiful don't convey that quality to the camera. Of course, basic physical characteristics are important. Good teeth, strong features, or beautiful eyes are great advantages, but ultimately a child must have that "special something" that makes people take a second look.

A child model should be able to act or role-play. A big part of modeling is "making believe;" the child has to put himself into a situation and convey the appropriate emotions to the photographer. For example, a child working on an advertisement for adhesive bandages may be asked to act hurt and unhappy, while a child doing a shoot with a wriggling puppy may be required to act happier than he's been all day! The best models are the ones who have almost instant access to their emotions, as well as the ability to access them on cue. They must be able to listen to and follow directions. The model is really more of an actor than you

Photo by Wilhelmina Models

would think, so if your child likes to "pretend" he certainly has an advantage.

Size is another factor that plays a very important part in the industry. Children that are small for their age actually have an advantage since they tend to be more mature than others of their size. A ten-year-old boy who looks two years younger will probably get more work than an eight-year-old of the same size. This is also a real ego booster for a child who has always been smaller than everyone else and a chance to prove his worth, though it may mean that the child isn't going to grow up to be a six-foot tall model. It's worth noting that being a child model does not guarantee modeling success as an adult.

The clothing size that a child wears also determines how much work is available in a given period of time. When clothing catalogs and advertisements are being produced, the clothing manufacturers supply clothing for the models in standard sample sizes. Child models who work in fashion or catalogs have to conform as closely as possible to the sizes that are provided. These sizes range from 12 to 24 months for babies and sizes 2 to 12 for children. The most popular sizes are generally 12 months, 5 and 10.

Photo by Wilhelmina Models

Clothes will look best on perfectly proportioned models, limiting the amount of work that a thin or overweight child can obtain.

All other sizes are called off-sizes. As kids grow it is common to have slow periods in which they receive less work while they are between sizes, although there are still modeling opportunities other than fashion or catalog work where size is less important.

What about teeth? If a child is temporarily missing a tooth, he will be fitted for a bridge or flipper, which fits inside the mouth like a denture and fills in the missing tooth. Flippers are very common among younger children who are often inclined to proudly pop them out and display them at go-sees and auditions. Braces, on the other hand, will generally limit the amount of work that a child gets, unless the casting director is specifically looking for a model with braces. But since straight teeth are a necessity, the time and money invested in braces are definitely worthwhile. You might want to consider braces that are attached to the inside of your child's teeth, although they must be worn for a longer time than regular braces. If your child's teeth are stained or discolored you may want to invest in a professional cleaning or whitening to restore their original brightness.

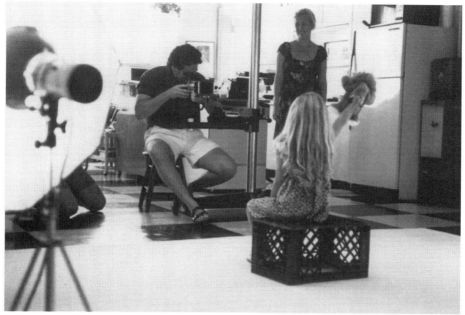

Photo by Randall Harris

Equal in importance to physical appearance is discipline. It doesn't matter what your child looks like if he or she can't follow directions or sit still for a prolonged period of time—sometimes hours on end. There are children in this business who disappear whenever the photographer turns away, who pout when they are given clothes that they don't want to wear—but they don't last very long. Modeling requires professionalism even from the very youngest talent. If your child comes home from school every week with a note from his teacher about misbehavior in class, perhaps you should think twice about modeling. Not only will an undisciplined child receive less and less work, but he won't enjoy the work.

The most important factor that will determine success is your child's desire to work in the modeling industry. He should be comfortable around strangers, outgoing, and able to follow direction. And, since he won't get every job he's up for, he should also be able to handle the inevitable rejection when it comes. How does he react when he loses or doesn't get his way?

There are a lot of parents who have a very hard time dealing with their child's rejection, and often it's easier for the child to handle it than the parents. But you should remember that your attitude

as a parent will affect the way your child deals with rejection. If you project disappointment when your child fails to get a job, it's going to make your child feel bad as well. But if you maintain a positive outlook, you can teach your child that there's nothing wrong with not getting every job, but rather it's just part of the business (and part of life). Sometimes a casting director or producer has a specific look in mind for a particular job, so no child, no matter how appealing, will get the job unless he conforms exactly to a preset image. There's a lot of pressure involved in the business, so think about whether your child (and you) can work in a fast-paced and competitive environment.

It may take a dozen auditions and go-sees before your child gets a great job. When rejection comes, handle it gracefully. Don't take it personally. And remember that the attitude you project is very important in helping your child learn to accept the low points as well as the high points in the business.

Chapter 3
Finding an Agency

Photo by Wilhelmina Models

I have explained that the modeling industry really is looking for all shapes and sizes in child models. Working child models represent the diversity of our society to a much greater extent than adult models, and, therefore, a very wide range of kids have a great chance of finding work. It doesn't matter if your child has blue or brown eyes, blond, black or red hair. Whether he or she is short or tall, African-American, Asian or Hispanic. This is a profession in which every kid has real opportunities if he or she has the desire and motivation to work as a model. Child modeling agencies get requests for overweight kids, athletic kids, even kids with disabilities such as Down's Syndrome. Unique traits are often an advantage.

So what's the first step toward making your child the next star? Since virtually all advertising companies, catalog companies, and magazines secure their models through agencies, you will have to find an agency to represent your child and obtain work for him or her.

Behind the Scenes

Most people have a pretty vague idea about what goes on behind the scenes of the modeling industry. Exactly who is it who puts

those bright and adorable kids in the ads that we see every day in magazines, on billboards, and on boxes containing everything from diapers to cereal to toys? You might think that individual companies select the kids that appear in their advertising and packaging. Some companies do, in fact, produce their own work, but the vast majority rely on outside companies to do the work. Large companies specialize. For example, Kodak makes film, Tonka makes toys, and Crayola makes crayons. These companies don't have the time or resources, however, to produce catalogs, advertising, and artwork. Instead, they rely on specialized companies that handle these different areas of work. These include advertising agencies, catalog production companies ("catalog houses"), graphic design companies, and others. It's up to modeling agencies, with their own resources and experience, to find the kids who appear in the ads and artwork that are produced by these companies. A modeling agency is the liaison between your child and the wide range of companies, from toy stores like Toys R Us to fashion retailers like Macy's and The Gap, that need to use children in advertisements and catalogs, and magazines and newspapers that need children for editorial work. It is the role of the booking agents ("bookers") at each agency to promote and find work for the children that the agency represents. In return

Photo by Randall Harris

for securing work for the child, the agency takes a percentage of the pay, usually somewhere between 15 and 25 percent. That's how they make money. You do not have to pay money for representation, nor for an interview or evaluation.

Let's take a look at what happens before a model appears in print. The example that follows is a description of everything that must occur before you see a model in a fall catalog of back-to-school clothes:

ABC Clothing Company has a great new line of children's clothes for the fall season. They are a mail-order company, so they need to put out a back-to-school catalog toward the end of summer to introduce the clothes to consumers. Because of the time involved in creating catalogs and advertising, it's only January now, but ABC has samples of every item going into the catalog and is ready to start work.

Like most companies, ABC hires an outside company to produce its catalogs. ABC supplies a sample of each item of clothing, and a catalog house is responsible for putting together the catalog. The first step for the catalog house is to contact agencies and give them brief descriptions of the kinds of kids they want to see for

Photo by Randall Harris

this particular catalog. Size is especially important, and the catalog house will be looking for models who wear standard sample sizes. The casting director will then call modeling agencies and ask them to send their most appropriate children to the studio on a go-see.

At the go-see the casting director, and often the client, get to see a range of children from which to select the most appropriate for the shoot. There may be anywhere from a half-dozen to 100 kids, depending on how many agencies have sent children. When the casting director has decided on the best models for the job, he or she will contact their agencies to book them.

The models must arrive promptly for the photography session, or shoot, which usually lasts for an hour or two. When the model arrives he signs in, providing his name, agency name, and the time of arrival. He then sees a make-up and hair stylist who applies any necessary make-up and then styles his hair. A fashion stylist makes sure that the model is well-dressed and accessorized, and that all of the clothes that the model is wearing fit correctly. Only after this work does the shoot begin.

Photo by Randall Harris

The photographer's studio is a large open space in a former warehouse. Lights suspended from the ceiling supplement the bright sunlight streaming in through large windows, and a huge fan provides a cooling breeze across the wooden floor. At one end of the studio, a large sheet of white canvas is hung to provide a neutral backdrop for the shoot. When the model arrives from the stylists, the photographer explains the idea for the photograph and positions him in front of the backdrop. Then the photographer measures the light levels, makes adjustments to the lighting, and focuses his camera on the model. "Okay, give me a smile and let's begin!"

Agents and Managers

The responsibilities of a modeling agent are diverse. First and foremost, the agent is responsible for representing and promoting the children at her agency. When a client calls to request models for an advertisement or editorial layout, the agent will send the models that best fit the requirements to the go-see. Over time a relationship is built between the clients and modeling agency. The agent learns what kind of children specific clients and photographers prefer to work with, and the client can trust the agent to send the most appropriate models.

Photo by Randall Harris

An agent is more than just someone you work with. She is also an adviser and a friend, a person who will share your successes when your child books a job and make it easier for you when a job doesn't come through.

An agent works for a single agency and is responsible for sending the best models on go-sees. A manager, on the other hand, takes a broader role in a child's career. The manager is the liaison between models and agencies, whether modeling or television, and helps guide the model's career. A child who is signed with a manager has access to a greater variety of jobs because the manager can send the child on go-sees through a number of agencies. Here's the way it works: A client calls an agency to request kids that are four years old with red hair. The agency may only have one model that fits the requirements, so they in turn call a manager to look for more kids that meet the same requirements. If the manager has someone, he will send the model to the go-see and take a percentage—about 15 percent of gross earnings—in addition to the percentage taken by the agency who submits the child. A manager is really only necessary when a child is well-established and working in a variety of media.

Chapter 4
Where are the Agencies?

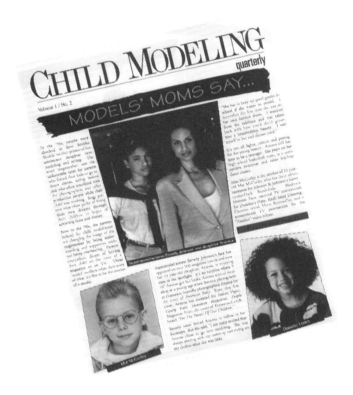

Where should you send your pictures? The best source for agency names is your local yellow pages, which will provide you with the names of agencies in your immediate area. There are also directories of agencies in specific regions; one example is the "Ross Report," an industry-produced listing of all of the modeling agencies in New York, along with the specific requirements for each agency. Additionally, agency directories for each state in the country are published and regularly updated by "Child Modeling Quarterly" newsletter.

When you think about it, it should come as no surprise that the modeling industry is concentrated in major cities such as New York, Los Angeles, Miami, Atlanta, Chicago, and Dallas. These cities are all strong markets for child models, and are home to major advertising agencies, publishers, and catalog producers. The established modeling agencies in these cities generally work with only those people who live within a reasonable commuting distance, generally less than two hours. It may seem unfair to those outside these metropolitan areas, but because this is such a fast-paced industry it is important that models can be almost instantly available when they are requested. For example, Wilhelmina may get a call from a client who wants to see three or

four kids as soon as possible. There's no time for parents to bring their children into the city if they live several hours away—by the time they arrive, the go-see will be over. Even parents who are determined to make the commute from far outside the city soon find that it's just not practical.

Additionally, a child who has to travel several hours for a single shoot is apt to be tired, cranky, and difficult to work with before the job has even started. Constant commuting is expensive. And you don't really want to spend that much time in the car, do you?

Chapter 5
First Contact

Photos by Wilhelmina Models

Modeling agencies that represent adults usually have open calls once or twice a week. This is a set time when aspiring models can come into the agency to introduce themselves and drop off pictures for consideration. For children, the procedure is different. Most child modeling agencies, at least the major ones, don't have open call days (imagine the chaos!). Instead, your first contact will be made through the mail.

There is a right way to approach agencies, and it's simple and quick. All you need is a set of good snapshots of your child and the addresses of modeling agencies in your area. You'll also need a little time and patience!

First, let's talk about the picture you're going to need to submit to the agencies. You absolutely do not need to get professional pictures made. They're often expensive and, since kids change so quickly, they will quickly be out of date. Don't let a photographer try to talk you into a $500 set of pictures at this point. An experienced modeling agent can tell just as much about your child from a candid home snapshot as from a professional studio portrait. You can take the picture yourself, provided you follow a few tips that will help you bring the best out of your child:

Photo by Wilhelmina Models

Shoot outside. Bright sunlight gives much better results than indoor lighting or flash. It also eliminates the "red-eye" that can result from flash pictures.

Take a vertical, rather than horizontal, picture. This allows more room for a full-length photo of your child. Your child should be centered, with the head in the upper third of the picture.

Only the child should be in the picture. No family portraits or groups of friends.

The child should wear bright colors and simple patterns. Avoid solid black and white, as well as overly trendy clothing.

The child should be neatly groomed. For babies, clean clothes and face. For boys, a fresh haircut, and for girls a simple hairstyle—and no make-up!

Use a recent picture. If it's the middle of the summer an agent does not want to see a picture of your child in front of the Christmas tree. He or she knows that a child's appearance can change a great deal in six months.

The expression on your child's face should convey a feeling that can be anything—lighthearted or serious, somber or thoughtful.

You want to capture his or her unique personality and show the agent something that will catch his attention.

After you've selected a favorite picture and made a few dozen copies, write the child's name, height, and date of birth on the back. Also include your address and telephone number. Send the picture with a brief cover letter stating your availability for an interview if the agency should desire. Send only photos—no slides, negatives, or videos. One enthusiastic parent recently sent Wilhelmina an entire photo album full of baby pictures! Please, just one or two pictures.

It takes about two weeks for the children's division of Wilhelmina to contact parents if we are interested in the child, though it may take other agencies as long as four to six weeks to contact you if they are interested in meeting you and your child. If there is not a need for your child at the time, however, you may not hear anything at all. Agencies generally will not return photographs unless you enclose a stamped, self-addressed envelope. They simply get too many inquiries—large agencies get thousands every year. But you shouldn't be discouraged yet, because there are many reasons that a child may get a rejection notice. His size may temporarily be an off-size, or the agency may simply have enough

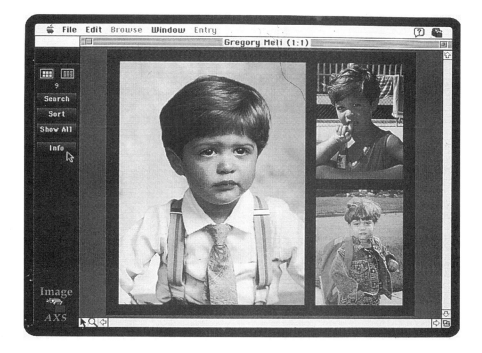

blond, blue-eyed five-year-olds at the time. Agency needs are always changing, and if your child is initially rejected by a particular agency you can resubmit a photograph four to six months later. It may take a lot of time and effort to find the right agency, but persistence will pay off.

On-Line Casting Services

The modeling industry is now going high-tech with the development of revolutionary on-line casting services that provide an alternative to mass mailing pictures to agents. These new services use the latest in computer and communication technologies to allow talent scouts, casting agents, and modeling agencies anywhere in the world to see a model's composite and biographical information at the touch of a button. They provide maximum exposure for models and actors and greatly simplify the work for anyone who needs an overview of available talent.

Here's how it works: For a fee, a model or other image provider, such as an actor, photographer, or stylist, subscribes to an on-line casting service such as New York-based UltimateSource. The casting service adds the model's picture and personal information in digital form to a database, which it then makes available to

Photo by Penny Gentien

image users, such as modeling and advertising agencies, across the country and around the world. This information is provided to image users either via regularly updated CD-ROMs, which are compact discs that hold visual information, or via telephone lines and modem. Using a personal computer, model and talent agencies can access the information to get an overview of new talent, or, by entering specific attributes, to find models that meet their specific needs.

For example, if a model agent wants an athletic blonde with green eyes for an advertising campaign, he can enter these qualifications into the system. The agent may also need to find models with specific talents or who live in a certain region. Once this information has been entered, the service will provide a list of models that fit these criteria, along with information on how to contact them.

The on-line casting services can also be used by others who rely on photographs to promote themselves. Stylists, hairdressers, and other image creators can also present examples of their work to agencies and other potential employers.

Photo by Wilhelmina Models

On-line systems insure maximum exposure for minimal cost. Information and pictures can be easily updated on the on-line networks, eliminating the need to conduct frequent mass mailings when information changes. Image providers are able to make their most recent work instantly available in a neat and organized format.

Chapter 6
Summer Kids and Other Opportunities

Photo by Bettina Countryman

What do you do if you live in the rural Midwest, Montana or Maine, yet are determined to pursue modeling? Is it possible? Absolutely! The models in New York and Los Angeles have come from across the country and around the world. Many agencies in New York and Los Angeles will consider a child whose parents are willing to commit to a certain length of time in the city, usually during the summer. "Summer kids" are a common part of many agency's rosters, complementing the models already signed with the agency. As one agency director says, "The children who are offered summer representation are chosen very carefully. We want to find children who are not competing with children that we already have. They all need to look different so that they will all be working."

Remember, it's very important that when you submit a picture to an agency in New York or Los Angeles you indicate when you can be available to move to the city and how long you can stay. If you don't, the picture will probably not get a second look.

Most summer kids come to New York with their mothers. Because of the high cost of living in the city, it's not uncommon for several mothers and children to share a single apartment. Several people, often from the same area, can therefore split the

Photo by Bob Cass

expenses of a summer in the Big Apple. Agencies may provide assistance in locating suitable housing, but they do not pay any rent or living expenses. While most children earn substantial incomes during the summer, no agency can guarantee that your child will earn enough to pay for your living expenses. You must be able to afford the possibility that you will only break even or possibly even lose money.

Before committing to a summer in New York (or any other major market such as Los Angeles or Miami) it's a good idea to look for work locally, no matter where you live. A New York agency is more likely to give consideration to a child who has successfully obtained work in his or her own area, even though the jobs will probably have been smaller.

Almost every region of the country has opportunities if you look for them. While the compensation will probably not be comparable to that in larger markets, local work gives you and your child the chance to get a feel for the business. It also gives your child valuable experience, and if you do obtain local work you'll have something to show when you contact major agencies. The money that you earn in the local market will also help finance your trips to bigger cities.

Photos by Wilhelmina Models

There are modeling agencies in many mid-sized cities across the country, but there are also other ways to get your feet wet. Anything that puts your child on a stage or in the middle of attention will help later in his or her career. You may want to get in touch with the special events coordinator at the major department stores in your area to find out if there are opportunities at local fashion shows. Local and regional stores produce advertising and may need models; contact the advertising departments and find out who does the work. You may also want to call local advertising agencies to find out who supplies the children that appear in their advertisements.

Chapter 7
Baby Models

Photo by John Fortunato

Photo by Corey Sipkin

Can you introduce a newborn baby to the world of modeling? Absolutely! One of the most fashionable accessories for a model today is a smiling baby in her arms. Many advertisers feel that babies help soften ads and give them a comical side, and they certainly appeal to the "thirty-something" generation, many of whom are now parents themselves.

Kate Pregano is the president of Pregano & Goya Marketing in Detroit, and does the casting for the famous Gerber Products company. "I look for lovable, healthy, happy babies with big smiles and big expressive eyes," says Kate. "Most kids are cute enough to model, but not all babies have the personality to be a successful model. On any set there are a lot of people, so the babies that model for Gerber have to be comfortable around a lot of people. We don't require babies to sit still for the entire shoot. On a set we use lots of fluffy toys for the children to play with. Bubbles are one of my favorite things to get a baby's attention.

The sets are huge, so the babies can crawl all over the place and we can capture them in natural looking poses. Parents are allowed on the set, and whenever possible I like to use a baby's real mother in advertisements. It gives the ads a warmer and more realistic feeling."

Photo by Andrea Bishof

Cathy Jennings, of Baby Wrangler in New York, has done casting for companies including Pampers, Huggies, Luvs, Playskool, and Fisher Price. She prefers children who can sit still for a period of time. "For print I look for babies who are patient and easily directable. I need babies who can do a specific activity many times with enthusiasm—happy babies with manageable energy. I also look for independent babies who can function without seeing their parents."

Cathy prefers that the parents not be on the set during a shoot. "The parents are in a separate room watching their baby on a television monitor. I want the baby to look at the model as if she were their natural mother. Sometimes when a baby sees his real mother he gets distracted and becomes more difficult to direct."

Chapter 8
What the Parents Say

Photo by Wilhelmina Models

Parents are an integral part of any child's modeling career. When they introduce their children to modeling they are, often unknowingly, also committing themselves to a new career—or several new careers! Parents of child models act in numerous capacities that include manager, tutor, accountant, and chauffeur—in short, whatever it takes to help their kids. They play an especially important role in a newborn baby's career since children at such a young age don't even realize that they're auditioning and modeling.

Valerie Miller, whose eight-month-old daughter Yvette did an American Express commercial, says of the experience, "I was able to communicate with my baby on a higher level than I thought possible. I used familiar cooing sounds and body language and Yvette did what I asked her to do. The commercial took two days to shoot and it was a great experience.

"All of my friends had told me bad things about the modeling business, but the people I work with are really sweet. I know a lot of people spend money on unnecessary pictures and classes. These horror stories could be avoided if the parents knew how the child modeling industry works.

"I do this strictly for fun. Modeling is not a job for Yvette or my other two daughters who model. But I think modeling has really enhanced my children's tendency to strive for something. We work very hard and it teaches them defeat with winning. I have never reprimanded them, and I always say better luck next time if they don't get a job."

Maureen Rademaker has three children who have been modeling since they were in diapers. "When I had my first son, Sean, I got a little bored of staying home every day, so I sent pictures of Sean to some reputable agencies. He was eleven months old at the time, and was invited for an interview by the children's division of Wilhelmina.

"The day we went to talk with the agents at Wilhelmina, they sent us on a go-see. There were hundreds of children and their parents in the waiting room. I even spoke with a mother who said she would never do this again because it was too crowded! But Sean got the job and appeared in the editorial pages of Healthy Kids magazine.

"Conner, my youngest child, worked when he was only six week sold for Tampax breast-feeding bras. At first I was a little

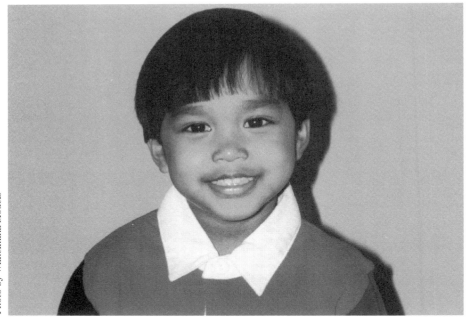

uncomfortable having a young model hold my child, but everyone who worked on the project was very accommodating to my needs as a mother, and the advertisement was tastefully done. For the entire shoot I was only inches away from Conner, and the photographer and model were continually asking me if they were holding my son properly or if I felt they were doing anything wrong. My husband Anthony even did a commercial with our daughter Erin, who was four months old at the time, for the investment banking company of Shearson & Lehman. They wanted a daughter being carried in a backpack by her real father. The whole family was there when they shot the commercial, and we had a great time.

"Modeling has really broadened my children's horizons. We live in the suburbs of Wilmington, Delaware, and drive two hours to New York for go-sees and work. Whenever we go to the city I make sure we do something fun, like going to the zoo, walking through the park, or window shopping at FAO Schwartz."

Maureen says that most jobs are tailored for the children who work on them. "Instead of adult food like salmon and shrimp scampi, they had an entire table with food for kids, including baby food, peanut butter and jelly sandwiches, and chocolate milk.

There are some jobs where there is only adult food, so it's always a good idea to bring your own food and snacks.

"The best advice that I can offer to parents who want their infants to model is that babies do not need professional pictures. I only use home snapshots of my three children, and they have modeled for hundreds of advertisements and catalogs. I also think it's better to start the children young. It was much harder for my son Sean to get into go-sees and auditions when he was eleven months old than it was for my other two children who started as infants." Children who start modeling very early will quickly become accustomed to the lights and stage environment, making it easier for them to work later on."

Chapter 9
What the Kids Say

You've heard parents talking about their experiences in the ever-changing but always exciting world of the child model's family. But the child models themselves have their own thoughts about the industry, and some of what they have to say may surprise you.

Mary Ellen Cravens is an outgoing eleven-year-old New Yorker who has modeled for Wilhelmina for about a year. She also acts, and has appeared on Broadway in "An Inspector Calls." Following is her very complete description of a go-see and a shoot.

"It's usually very busy at the go-see! When you arrive, you have to sign in, giving your name and the name of your agency. You show the casting director your book, which has examples of the work you've done, and then you give them your picture so they'll remember you. The casting director will ask your height, shoe size, age, and then looks through your book. You go into a room with other girls and try on the clothes—sometimes they're too big, so you roll them up! Finally you have your picture taken in the clothes.

"The casting director and the client then decide who gets the job. It depends on how well the clothes fit and how you get along. Sometimes you get it, and sometimes you don't."

Justin Pierre

Photo by Wilhelmina Models

What happens if you get the job?

"The shoot is usually in a studio. They have great music on when you arrive, and you are given your clothes and maybe shoes and socks to put on. Next you go to the hair and make-up people and stylists, and this is really fun. They put make-up on you, and sometimes lipstick and eye shadow. Then they try to decide how to style your hair, and ask how you how you usually do it. The stylists also give you accessories and jewelry to go with your outfit.

"When you're finished getting ready you go out and see the client who you're doing the shoot for. They will either say you look great, or make suggestions about changes to your hair and styling—but usually they think you look fine.

"At the shoot, the photographer will give you directions while you're standing in front of a backdrop—for example, 'put your hands on top of your head' or 'cross your legs' or just 'go on your own.' He might even ask what kind of music you want to hear, since they have a lot of music. I ask for Mariah Carey! When the music is on it helps, because at first you're kind of stiff, but when you hear music you're moving around, doing poses, and smiling a lot.

Photos by Jade Albert

"I've done print work for clients including Vogue, Hyatt Hotels, and Esprit, and commercials for Berry Berry Kix cereal, Lysol, the Red Cross, and lots of others.

"The best part of modeling is that you get to meet a lot of different people and you feel like you're important. All of the people are really nice, and it feels like modeling is a second home."

Nine-year-old Pierce Cravens is also an experienced Wilhelmina Model and, like his sister, has also appeared in commercials for companies including Tide, Era, and Sears. Pierce is currently on Broadway as an understudy in "Beauty and the Beast." He enjoys meeting and working with the wide variety of people in the industry, even when he's very busy.

"In the summer I go to about three go-sees a day. It's so busy that we hardly have time to sit down!" Sometime the work can be tiring, too. "Once for a Sesame Street advertisement I had to stand still and hold a sandwich for two hours."

Child models like Pierce demonstrate that it's possible to work and still have enough time to do other things. He finds time to pursue a variety of other activities such as hockey and sports programs.

Photo by Wilhelmina Models

Mary Ellen and Pierce make it clear that success and having fun go hand-in-hand in the child modeling industry. You'll find that everything possible is done to make the work as comfortable and fun as it can be for the kids and their parents.

Chapter 10
Industry Scams

Photo by Wilhelmina Models

One of the most difficult aspects of entering the industry is finding a reputable agency. It's a process that is full of potential risks for the uninformed parent who is drawn to the idea of making his or her child a model and, after spending hundreds of dollars, ends up with nothing more than a poor set of photographs. Stories about rip-off artists are far too common, and have the unfortunate result of giving many people a negative impression of the industry.

The modeling industry has the unfortunate position of being one of the businesses most attractive to scam artists and other shady characters. Why? Because parents with stars in their eyes are often all too willing to part with huge sums of money—up to $1,000 is not uncommon—to pursue the dream of putting their kids in the spotlight.

How do you avoid these unscrupulous operators? First, remember how a legitimate agency works; no money changes hands until a child has secured work, and at that point the agency receives only a percentage of the money earned by the child for the shoot. It doesn't work any other way.

MODELS WANTED! Earn $1000s per day—no experience needed! We're looking for all ages and types! Call today at (212) 555-2244

Spotting con artists preying on the dreams of children and their parents is not very difficult. There are a few very common methods these bogus agencies use to lure in prospective models and swindle their money.

Often, newspaper advertisements promise hundreds of dollars per day with no experience for "all types and ages." When the prospective parent brings his or her child in, the agent is ecstatic about the prospects for this child with unquestionable potential. "There's going to be a fantastic demand for the child," says the agent, "but first we need to expose the child to prospective clients. And to do this we need photos." You don't know how to find a photographer? Well, the agent is eager to recommend one.

The agent then goes on to explain that the company can open doors for the child just as long as they have appropriate pictures to show clients. Of course, the agency recommends a photographer who charges hundreds of dollars and then shares the profit with the agency, unknown to the parent. If you think this sounds unfair, you're right. It's an illegal kickback. In some cases, the agency will also recommend overpriced modeling or acting classes, again from associated talent schools.

Photo by Wilhelmina Models

When you see ads in newspapers, remember: there are thousands of people who want to get into the modeling industry. The top agencies receive thousands of pictures and calls from hopeful parents each year, and simply don't need to advertise for talent.

Another common scheme comes from firms that charge people hundreds or even thousands of dollars to be listed in their "talent directories," which are then mailed to agents and producers. It seems like a great way to be seen, but in reality, most agents don't even glance at these directories. The vast majority of directories end up in the trash as unopened dreams.

What is the end result? Usually nothing but disillusionment. So why do these scams continue to flourish? In many cases, people don't realize that they've been conned. They wait for the phone to ring, thinking that their kids just don't have what it takes. They are often young, naive, and not inclined to complain.

There are several ways for parents to protect themselves from scams. First, you should immediately be wary of anyone who asks for money up front. This warning sign alone is enough to tell you to keep looking. Second, check with the Better Business Bureau in your city. They have extensive records on hundreds of agencies

Photo by Wilhelmina Models

across the country and will tell you whether an agency has a satisfactory rating, based on the number of complaints that they have received against each agency.

The bottom line? If it sounds too good to be true, it probably is.

Chapter 11
The First Interview

Photo by Wilhelmina Models

Photo by Randall Harris

After reviewing the dozens of pictures that it receives every week, an agency will choose the kids that it feels show the greatest modeling potential and invite them for personal interviews. Wilhelmina's children's division, for example, interviews six to eight children per week. If you get a call expressing interest, you've got your foot in the door! It means that the agent has seen something about your child that stands out from the rest and makes him want to see more. Remember that the interview will be your only opportunity to create the all-important first impression.

When you visit a major agency for the first time, you'll find yourself in the midst of a storm of activity. The phones are constantly ringing with calls requesting children for shoots, children and parents are waiting for interviews, last-minute schedules are being made and changed, and it seems that there are a dozen crises about to happen. It's all part of the excitement and energy of the industry. You can make your child's interview a more pleasant experience for everyone involved by making sure that you are prepared and acting in a professional manner.

How should you groom your child before the interview? Stick as closely as possible to the appearance in the picture you sent in

since it's obviously a look that the agency liked. This isn't the time to experiment with new hairstyles or clothing trends. Your child should be dressed in casual and neat attire that is clean and not heavily worn. When asked, most agents will automatically tell you that the all-American "Gap" look—jeans and a T-shirt or button-down shirt—is always a safe bet for interviews and go-sees. It's a look that stays stylish without being trendy. Keep in mind that new clothes may make a child uncomfortable, so stick to something familiar.

Hair should be kept simple for both boys and girls. An extremely long, short, or trendy haircut will limit the possible number of "looks" that a child can adopt and will weigh against your child at the interview. The haircut should not be too new; a haircut that is a week or two old will give your child a much more natural appearance.

Young girls should not wear makeup, and for teens it is best to wear as little as possible. Girls should not try to appear older than they are. Agencies and clients want to see kids that look their age.

Make sure that you arrive promptly for the interview, giving yourself time for any last-minute delays. Punctuality is of the utmost

Photo by Wilhelmina Models

importance in the industry, and arriving late will immediately give the agency a bad first impression.

The interview will probably last for 10 or 15 minutes. Your child should be prepared to sit still for at least this amount of time and (if old enough) to talk to the agent. This is a time for the agent to determine how outgoing the child is, so encourage your child to give detailed answers to any questions the agent asks. Questions for children of various ages may include:

What is your name?

How old are you?

Where do you live?

Do you like to have your picture taken?

What do you like to study?

What do you want to do when you grow up?

The agent will also be taking this opportunity to ask you questions as well. It's important to find out how motivated you are, how much you know about the business, and how flexible your schedule is. Remember, if your child is signed, you are both going to be very

Photos by Caliope / Deborah Feingold

busy! Following are some of the questions an agent may ask a parent at the interview:

Is your child currently signed with an agency?

Do you work?

How flexible is your schedule?

Does your child participate in many extracurricular activities?

Are you familiar with the city?

Will you be able to invest a minimal amount of money ($50 to $100) for pictures and daily expenses such as commuting without a guaranteed return?

It is unusual for an agent to sign your child on the first visit. A contract is like a marriage—you want to see how the relationship works before you make a final commitment. At Wilhelmina there is a trial period of four to six weeks during which an agent can see how clients are responding to the child. This can be determined, in part, by how often the model books a job after being sent on a go-see. The trial period also allows the child and parent a chance to get a feel for the industry. Modeling requires a great deal of

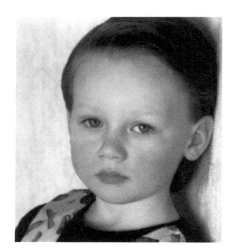

Photo by Bob Cass

motivation, time, and even money (for tolls, transportation, parking, etc.), and many parents had expected something very different. If a parent has serious time constraints or transportation difficulties, it will be very difficult to commit to the demands of a modeling career. There will also be some children who are not comfortable with the energy and fast pace of the industry, and choose not to continue modeling.

In some cases the child may be signed immediately following the interview, but this usually only occurs when the child has already had experience in the industry and is changing from one agency to another.

After the trial period Wilhelmina will evaluate the child's history with the agency and make a decision about whether to continue representation.

Some children will not, at the close of the trial period, be offered a contract. There are many possible reasons, but above all it will be because of a lack of response from clients. Wilhelmina, like other reputable agencies, will not continue representation if regular work does not seem likely. We want the modeling experience to be a positive one for every child signed.

Photo by Bob Cass

Finally, the interview will give you a chance to ask any questions you may have. Especially at a smaller agency, there are several questions you may want to ask. If there are examples of work on the wall, find out if the agency does in fact represent the models and obtained the work for them. You might ask how many children the agency represents, and ask to see some example of their recent work. Note the level of activity in the office. Are the phones ringing off the hook, or is the atmosphere quiet and subdued? In this business, a little chaos is a good sign!

Chapter 12
Tools of the Trade: What You'll Need

Photo by Jade Albert

Getting signed with an agency is the first real step in your child's new career. You are on your way to work! First, however, you will have to make a few small investments.

When your child is signed, your new agent will take some time to explain the expenses you will need to incur to get your child's career off the ground. It won't be much, but it is important that you take the time to prepare well.

The single most important tool of the trade in modeling is the professional photograph—also known as the composite, headshot, or test shot—that will be sent to prospective clients in order to market and secure work for the model. Once your child is signed by an agency you will have to provide this picture, and it must be updated—every six months for young models and annually for older ones—so that the agency always has a recent representation of the model.

An agency may choose to send your child to a test photographer to have the first pictures made. A test photographer will take your child's pictures for a very low fee—usually just enough to cover film processing—or even without charge, because in exchange he has the chance to experiment with new lighting and sets, and can

Photo by Jade Albert

use the photographs in his personal portfolio. If you don't go to a test photographer you will have to pay for the photographs and composites. The expense depends on the photographer and the type of pictures you want; a set of snapshots is far more economical than a glossy set of composite cards. The agency will tell you which kind of picture it prefers.

Another necessity of the modeling industry is an answering machine, second in importance only to the model's picture. If you don't already have one, you should definitely make the investment. Your agency must be able to reach you at any time. If you're away from your home for an extended time it's advisable to check your messages frequently so that you don't miss any go-sees. If your agency is unable to reach you on a regular basis, it will eventually be less inclined to try to contact you about work.

Your child will need a good basic wardrobe to work in the industry. For fashion and editorial shoots, the model wears clothing provided by the client, but for product ads the model usually wears his or her own clothes. The agency will tell you the general look that the client wants, but you still need to bring a variety of outfits to choose from at the time of the shoot. These clothes should only be worn for modeling so that they are always clean

Photo by Jade Albert

and fresh. The following articles should be packed in a bag and taken to every assignment:

For boys:

White tennis shoes

Dress shoes

Navy, brown, black and white socks

Assorted belts

For girls:

White tennis shoes

Dress shoes

Assorted white socks

Bobby pins and barettes

And for both:

Toothpaste and toothbrush

Comb and brush

Photos by Wilhelmina Models

Concealer for blemishes and scrapes

Clips and masking tape for last-minute alterations

A favorite toy

The client will let you know before a shoot if the child should bring any other clothing or props or items of clothing.

The Portfolio

When your child has completed several jobs, it will be time to create a portfolio. The portfolio, known as a "book" in the industry, is a case that holds photographs of the model along with examples of his or her work. These examples, called tearsheets, are taken directly from the magazine or catalog in which they appeared. You should keep copies of all print work that your child has appeared in. These samples are more valuable than test photographs since they prove to a client that the model has successfully obtained previous work. Portfolios may be purchased at art supply stores for less than $50, though some agencies supply their own with the agency name on the cover.

Chapter 13
Modeling Schools and Pageants

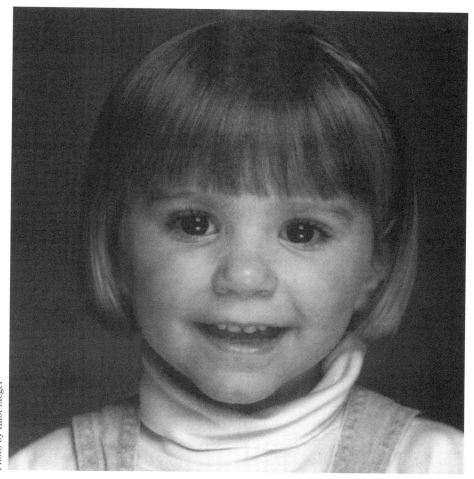

Photo by Eliot Siegel

Photo by Wilhelmina Models

It seems like modeling schools far outnumber modeling agencies, especially outside the major markets. Tuition and materials often total several hundred dollars, but what do the schools really teach, and are they necessary?

For most children the answer is no. Schools and academies cannot teach the essential personality traits and attitude that make great models. They cannot change the essential appearance of a child. Modeling schools can, however, help a shy child become more comfortable in front of others and teach him or her confidence and poise.

For some children, modeling schools provide an introduction to the industry and serve to excite and motivate them. The school may bring out wonderful characteristics in a child; the child may find that he or she loves being on the stage. Unfortunately, however, there are modeling schools that accept children that have very little chance of being models. No amount of money can buy success or make a child photogenic.

Beauty and talent pageants provide a lot of glittery fun and excitement for families across the country. They are big business, too—but they have little to do with the world of modeling, even though

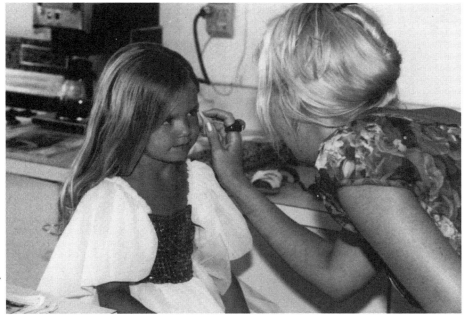

Photo by Randall Harris

they have changed considerably in the past few years. Many pageants now focus on speaking ability and performing arts as well as beauty. Still, a child who has been competing for years may have extra poise and confidence, but otherwise there is no real advantage for those children who have been active in pageants.

If your child is currently involved in pageantry, there are some important differences between pageants and the modeling industry that you should keep in mind. While make-up for pageants is usually elaborate and glamorous, even for the youngest contestants, it should be kept to a minimum for modeling interviews and go-sees. The same can be said for clothing and grooming: Pageantry is glitz and glamour, while models should always maintain a simple appearance that can be changed to meet the needs of a specific shoot.

As a parent, you will ultimately have a greater effect on your child and his or her performance than any school or pageant.

Chapter 14
The Work

Photos by Jade Albert

As a parent, it is your responsibility to call your child's agency on a daily basis to find out if there are any go-sees for your child to go on. It's also good to stay in touch with your child's agency to let it know you're available and ready to work.

The variety of work that child models can do is incredible. Just think of all the places you've seen them: in magazines and catalogs, of course, but also on billboards, boxes, books, and dozens of other places! The possibilities are limitless and depend only on the particular needs of the client. You should know about the primary categories of work:

Print

Over half of all child modeling is in the area of print work. The majority of print work is for children's fashions and clothing, and appears in media such as newspaper advertising, newspaper inserts, catalogs, and brochures.

Because of the look required, fashion is the most competitive area of child modeling. Companies want the children who will best show off their clothes, children who are thin, have a perfect size and beautiful faces.

National Advertising

About one-quarter of child modeling work is for national advertising, as hundreds of major companies use child models in advertising campaigns that are seen across the country. Gerber might be the first company that comes to mind, but there are many others, most that are not even selling products or services for babies or children! Looking through a magazine recently, I saw child models in advertisements for refrigerators, cameras, banks, vacation resorts, TV dinners, and half a dozen different kinds of cars.

Children in national campaigns for products don't have to conform to certain sizes or appearances, and, in fact, advertisers want kids who won't upstage their products! For this reason a child who is between sizes or doesn't have the "All-American" look may find plenty of opportunity to work.

Advertisers like to use children because they soften images and appeal to a segment of the population that is making a lot of major purchases—parents. If a parent sees a baby in an auto ad, he or she is given the impression of safety. A child in a bank ad may remind parents that they should begin investing for their child's

Photos by Jade Albert

future. Ads that feature child models also suggest that their products are "kid friendly"—that's important for parents.

Editorial

Editorial print work appears on magazine covers and accompanies articles in magazines or newspapers. Rather than selling a specific product or service, editorial work provides information of use to the reader. For example, a feature on back-to-school fashions would be accompanied by photographs of kids wearing the clothes mentioned in the article, and a story about trends in hairstyles might be accompanied by pictures of child models with the latest cuts. But editorial work is not limited to fashion. Photographs of children appear with articles about children and families and in public-service messages for children and their parents about childhood safety and concerns.

Other

The different kinds of work in this category are limited only by the imagination of art directors, and include everything from boxes and packaging to billboards and posters.

Photo by Wilhelmina Models

Television Commercials

Working on television commercials is a natural progression for many child models. Payment for national spots—the ads that are seen across the country on major networks—can be tremendous, because in addition to being paid for the shoot itself, the actors receive payment each time the commercial airs. Every time you see a commercial on TV, the actors are getting another check! These residuals can easily amount to tens of thousands of dollars over the life of a commercial.

Since modeling entails a certain amount of acting, many child models find it easy to make the transition into commercials. Of course, there are additional requirements for children who want to start working in commercials. They must have a good memory and, for older children, strong reading skills. At many auditions, a child will be asked to read a piece of commercial copy for the casting director, which he must read convincingly as if he really loves whatever product he's talking about!

Training for young actors is not as important as creativity and natural talent. Acting in commercials is different than acting in television or film. It requires spontaneity and the ability to role-play.

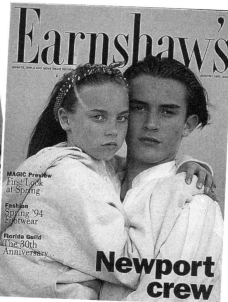

Children under ten rarely need formal training, since what they have to offer is their own unique personality. While formal training is not a requirement, there are many short courses that teach the basics of auditioning and acting. New York and Los Angeles have dozens of these classes, lasting a few weeks, which can be found listed in trade publications such as Backstage. They focus mainly on how the child can best prepare for an audition and what the process will be like—in short, these classes teach the child how to land parts as well as basic acting techniques.

The current rate of pay for a commercial is $414.25 per eight-hour day, although this rate is subject to frequent change. Most commercials take about two days to complete. The big money, of course, is in residuals. The rate of pay for residuals varies according to the number of times it is shown, the size of the market in which it is shown, the length of commercial, and the time of day. A commercial that airs during prime time in New York will pay higher residuals than one airing at midnight in West Texas. At First Global Management in New York, for example, there are children making as much as $200,000 per year because they have worked on commercials that are being frequently aired in major markets.

Photo by Penny Gentien

You don't have to be in a big city for your child to break into commercial acting, but if you live in a smaller town you will have to do a little more groundwork to find the opportunities. Get in touch with local advertising agencies (listed in the phone book) and find out if they shoot commercials in your area. Talk to the casting director or whoever does the casting and tell him or her about your child.

Chapter 15
The Business Side

Photo by Wilhelmina Models

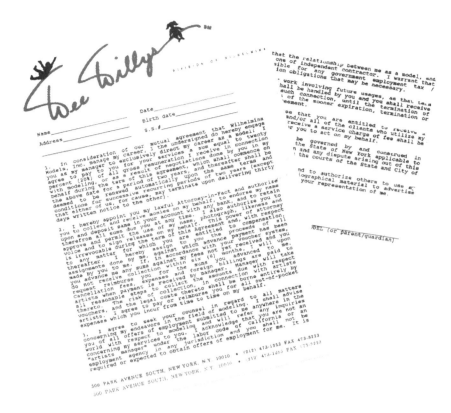

The Contract

After all of the pictures in the mail, the interviews, and the waiting, your child will eventually be offered a contract with an agency. A contract is a mutual agreement between the model and the agency, which sets forth the terms under which the model is to be represented. This is the moment you've been waiting for, but, as always, be sure to read every word before you sign anything.

While every agency has a different contract, we can look at the Wilhelmina contract to give you a good idea of what to expect at most agencies. Following are some of the most important terms.

A Wilhelmina contract is exclusive, which means that only Wilhelmina will manage and direct the career of the model. Other agencies, especially in smaller markets, may not have exclusive contracts. If this is the case, you are free to sign with several agencies, although eventually you will probably choose to work with only the one that obtains the most work for your child. All agencies in New York and California offer only exclusive contracts, while in Florida both exclusive and nonexclusive contracts are offered.

Photo by Wilhelmina Models

Under the Wilhelmina contract, the model agrees to pay the agency 20 percent of all gross earnings received in connection with modeling. This is a standard percentage. The standard contract is valid for a two-year period, although it can be terminated by either the model or agency with delivery of 30 days written notice with sufficient cause. There must be a valid reason for termination of the contract. For example, an agency may decide to end its relationship with a model who is often late for go-sees or bookings, fails to provide the agency with up-to-date pictures, or is generally uncooperative and difficult to work with. The agency may also terminate the contract of a model who has not been receiving a positive response from clients.

Parents may terminate a contract to change agencies, because they feel their child has not been getting enough work, or because they no longer wish to work in the industry.

Under the terms of the contract, the model authorizes the agency to use his or her name, photograph, likeness, and voice, and to sign releases on his or her behalf.

THE UNIVERSITY OF THE STATE OF NEW YORK
THE STATE EDUCATION DEPARTMENT
ALBANY, NEW YORK 12234

CHILD MODEL PERMIT

Valid for the employment of a minor under eighteen (18) years of age in the occupation of child model.   **Expires One Year From Date of Issuance**

PERMIT NUMBER	DATE OF ISSUANCE
NAME OF MINOR	
DATE OF BIRTH	SOCIAL SECURITY NUMBER
SIGNATURE OF MINOR (12 years of age or over), in presence of issuing officer	
ADDRESS OF ISSUING OFFICE	SIGNATURE of Issuing Officer for Chancellor

BE/ATT 7007 (Rev 6/92) ceinstr dsk 1

"Not proof of Employment Authorization Under I.R.C. Act of 1986."

Model Permit

Every child model under eighteen is required to obtain a work permit, which must be taken to every print job. The permit assures employers that the model is in good health and able to work. In New York City it is available free of charge from the Board of Education. You must apply in person with a copy of the child's birth certificate, Social Security number, and a note from a doctor stating that the child is in good health. Your agency will provide you with information about getting the permit in your area.

Vouchers

A voucher is one of the most important forms for a model. It is provided by the agency and is used to document the time a model arrives at and leaves a shoot, as well as the agreed-upon rate of pay. Vouchers produce three copies: one for the client, one for the model, and one for the agency. When completed and signed, the voucher must be sent or handed to the agency in order for the model to receive pay for work. Without a voucher, a model may have to wait until the agency receives payment from the client before he or she receives payment.

Wilhelmina
MODELS INC.

(212) 473-0700
300 Park Avenue South
New York, NY 10010
FAX (212) 473-3223

W₂

SEND
INVOICE
TO:

ADDRESS:
CITY
STATE   ZIP CODE

ATTENTION:

SPECIAL BILLING/P.O. #:

AGENCY COPY
(AS ATTORNEY IN FACT FOR)

MODEL NAME:			
DATE OF JOB:		USAGE	
PRODUCT		STUDIO	
RATE	TIME: FROM:	TO:	$
FITTING FEE	FITTING DATE		$
TRAVEL TIME:			$
MISC. EXPENSES			$
AGENCY FEE TO BE ADDED TO THE TOTAL AMOUNT. CHARTER MEMBER OF IMMA			
		TOTAL	$

UNIFORM MODEL RELEASE (VALID UPON PAYMENT)

In consideration of receipt of the model fee (inclusive of service fee) as well as any additional usage fees negotiated with my manager, I hereby sell, assign and grant to
_____
Advertising Agency or Publication   and _____ Client/Advertiser
the right and permission to copyright and use or publish one (1) photograph or likeness of me in which I may be included in whole or part of composite or reproductions thereof
in color or otherwise in the United States for _____ usage; i.e. Print, POS, Pkg, OOH, etc. for _____ months to
begin no later than four (4) months later than this date, except that these photos may not be used on TV in any manner. Accordingly, I release and discharge the company
and persons named above and persons acting for or on behalf of them from any liability by virtue of any blurring, distortion, alteration, optical illusion, or use in composite
form that may occur or be produced in the taking of said pictures or in any processing thereof through completion of the finished product. Note: Products, packaging usage,
billboards, point-of-sale, hang tags, exclusivity, endorsements, use of name, TV and any other special usage require separate negotiations. All other releases not valid unless
countersigned by model manager. Client's workman's compensation carrier is _____

CLIENT'S SIGNATURE _____ MODEL'S SIGNATURE _____

Taxes

Child models must have a Social Security number and will pay taxes at the same rates as adults. Just like an adult, any child model who earns more than $600 in a given year must report the income to the IRS. The model must file separately from his parents—essentially, under the law, a child model's earnings are treated just like those for an adult in almost every respect.

Be sure to save all of your receipts for all work-related expenses. Once your child has started to work, he or she is considered a professional, and as such all expenses related to work, including everything from travel to composites and postage, are tax-deductible. If your child is successful, you will probably want to work with an accountant who has experience in the entertainment industry.

Chapter 16
Go-Sees

Photo by Bob Cass

A go-see is essentially an audition for a model. If you end up working in New York or another strong market, you'll find that go-sees soon become a daily part of life—and after all the time you spend in taxis, you're going to know the city streets like the back of your hand! This is a time-consuming but necessary and unavoidable aspect of the industry.

It's important to remember that getting signed by an agency doesn't automatically mean getting work. The money comes from successfully booking, or obtaining, a job. For every job that is available, a client wants to see a variety of models so that they can choose the one that best fits their needs. This means that whenever your agency sends your child on a go-see, there will be several other kids up for the same job. Like an audition, the go-see is the child's only chance to make the all-important first impression. When an advertising agency, magazine, or other client needs a child model, they will call the agency to send a variety of models to their studio for the go-see. This gives them the opportunity to select the child that they feel best fits the demands of a particular shoot.

The decision about which models to use is generally made by a casting director, the person responsible for booking (selecting

Photo by Lou Freeman

and hiring) models for a shoot. The casting director screens out the models who are not right for a particular job while keeping an eye out for the ones that seem to be perfectly suited for it. The final decision is based on a number of factors, but the one that you have the most control over is your child's level of professionalism. A prepared child will always have a distinct advantage at a go-see.

Go-sees may be well-organized and quiet, but usually you'll find something more like a chaotic cattle call since many agencies may have sent models conforming to the casting director's requirements to vie for the same job. Open calls are the busiest go-sees, as they are open to any model who fits a very basic set of requirements such as age and height.

Sometimes a go-see is followed by a call-back. Once the casting director has reviewed the models seen at the go-see, he or she may want to see the most promising models again before making a final decision. When a model is asked to come to a call-back, it indicates strong interest on the part of the client.

Chapter 17
Payday

Photo by Tim Harper

Photo by Wilhelmina Models

It's a pleasant surprise to find that most families enter the industry not for fame and glamour, but to save for their child's future. Even though the public perception tends to be that the modeling industry is all about money and glamour, the truth is that most parents really are much more concerned with providing for their children than trying to get into the spotlight. In fact, saving for college is the number one concern for the parents of most child models. College costs are climbing every year, so it's never too early to start saving!

What kind of earnings can you and your child expect, and how much does a typical child model earn in a year?

Models are paid by the hour for their work. The minimum time that can be billed for is an hour, so even if a job takes only ten minutes the model will be paid for the full hour. The average rate of pay for a child model in New York is about $75 per hour for print work. For high exposure work such as billboards or packaging, the rate is up to five times the hourly rate, whereas work for catalogs and advertising in newspapers generally pays less because the volume of work is higher, so you can expect rates that are closer to $50 or $60 per hour. In smaller markets the pay will be accordingly less—and in every market there will be a great

Photo by Gordon Bass

deal of variation. Editorial work may pay anywhere from $25 to $100 per day, and as a sort of "trade-off" models will work for lower rates when they are getting work, such as a magazine cover, that will result in more future bookings.

There are no residuals for print work, which means that the model is paid only once for a shoot, no matter how many times a particular photograph is used within the normally negotiated 12-month period.

Successful children may earn anywhere up to $10,000 in a year or more. These models, however, are those who are working almost daily, and it's almost impossible to predict how much a given child will make in any year.

Chapter 18
Interviews With Industry Professionals

Photo by Jade Albert

Following are interviews with models and professionals working in every aspect of the child modeling industry. These are voices of experience.

JADE ALBERT, PHOTOGRAPHER

Jade Albert is a noted photographer based in New York. She took time out of her busy schedule to answer our questions about her work and the child modeling industry.

Q: What do you do?

A: I'm a photographer specializing in photographing children. I was the first photographer to usher in high-fashion sense to kid's advertising. I didn't capture children with big toothy grins, but rather I introduced images of children who are very sophisticated and adult-like. I'm well-known for photographs such as a boy wearing his father's blazer or a girl wearing her mother's sweater.

Q: What clients have you worked for?

A: Kids R Us, Sony, Polaroid, Huggies, Procter & Gamble, Saks Fifth Avenue, Macy's, Bloomingdales, Walt Disney, Johnson & Johnson, Tyco Toys, and Lever Brothers, among others.

Q: How did you get started photographing children?

A: I was a photographer for Vogue in Europe. They accidentally saw some personal photographs of my friends' children and decided to have me shoot their back-to-school catalog. The high-end fashion photos in the Saks catalog were revolutionary in the children's photography field and were very popular.

Q: Do you choose the children for a client?

A: I do open calls, which means that any child can show up at a go-see. I'm always looking for new kids. At the open call, I narrow down the number of children for the client, but the client has the final decision on which children to use for the catalog or advertisement.

Q: What characteristics are you looking for in the children you use?

A: The kids have to have a lot of stamina. Modeling is hard work. For one picture, kids may have to do something over and over again until I see what I like. They have to be disciplined and able to take directions easily. But one feature I look at most is the child's eyes. In one glance a child's eyes can show their character and personality.

Photos by Jade Albert

Q: How do you get the children to act like kids?

A: I treat them like friends. I don't lecture them. I play games and talk to them one-on-one. Since the children I work with trust me, they can act naturally for a shoot.

Q: What happens when a child is on the set and starts to cry?

A: I start crying too, and then the child begins to laugh. I send them back to hair and make-up, and we resume the shoot. If the child is tired, I usually have back-ups.

Q: What is a back-up?

A: A back-up is another child who can also do the shoot. I take pictures of all the back-ups, and the client chooses the child they like best. For children ages newborn to three, I always have three or four other children who can do the shoot. Babies, especially, need back-ups because they typically last for only one hour on a photo session, and if I'm shooting a national advertisement I can't afford to have a baby get tired or start teething.

Q: What's the best thing about working with children?

A: I enjoy photographing kids because they're so natural and they don't have attitudes or big egos.

Q: What suggestions would you give to parents who want to see their child in front of your camera for a national advertisement?

A: The child has to be natural and comfortable with modeling. Don't groom the child for a go-see the way you would for the Miss America Pageant. Natural hair and comfortable clothing is the best bet.

MARILYN ZITNER, TALENT MANAGER

Marilyn is a talent manager with First Global Management in New York.

Q: What do you do?

A: I'm a talent manager. I represent children and young adults for theater, movies, television shows, and commercials. I'm the liaison between the talent and the agents, casting directors, and producers. Unlike an agent who fills slots in interviews with the best talent for the job, I guide acting careers and give advice on everything from the selection of an acting coach and preparation for auditions to picking a new hairstyle an recommending a dentist.

Photo by Jade Albert

Q: What recent jobs have you gotten for children?

A: Hundreds of jobs, including those for Macy's, Cheerios, Oscar Meyer, Hasbro, Kellogg, Parker Brothers, Lipton, and Lego. Nine-year-old Lenny Spinelli just booked a TV pilot show called Gabby for NBC and Warner Brothers, and ten-year-old Craig Lawlor is now touring the country in the musical Tommy.

Q: How did most of the kids at First Global begin working with you?

A: A lot of children came to me through modeling agencies. Others sent me home snapshots, and if I liked the photographs, I invited them in for an interview.

Q: When you interview children for television, what are you looking for?

A: I'm looking for the child that you can't stop watching—the child that you can't take your eyes off. There's no one best look. Successful children have some sort of spark and a lot of charisma, and they're usually very talkative and outgoing. I'm also looking at the parents, making sure they aren't threatening the children to "do it—or else!" I want to make sure the parent isn't trying to live vicariously through the child, or looking for a quick buck.

Photos by Wilhelmina Models

Q: From the first audition, how long does it take for a child to land a TV commercial?

A: Getting a TV commercial is a very quick process. You can go on the first audition and two weeks later shoot the commercial. But TV shows and movies take much longer. It can take three months or more to audition, meet with producers and directors, and take a screen test.

Q: How much do some of these children make?

A: One of my children made $80,000 on a single Crest commercial. Four of the children that I manage are in a Cheerios commercial—they've each made $30,000 to date, and the commercial is still running.

Q: Do you have any suggestions for parents who want to get their kids involved in television?

A: I would suggest a mass mailing of pictures to managers and agents. Kids don't need professional pictures at first. An animated home snapshot of the child is fine. Go into the business with a fun attitude, and remember that kids should enjoy being kids. There must be a healthy balance between work and play.

SARA FELDMAN, FASHION EDITOR

Sara is a fashion editor at Parenting Magazine in New York.

Q: What do you do?

A: I'm the contributing fashion editor at Parenting Magazine. My responsibilities include covering the entire children's wear market and selecting the clothes for both kids and adults. I also produce all of the fashion editorials.

Q: Are you responsible for booking the models for your photo shoots?

A: Yes, I book all the child models for the fashion pages.

Q: Do you have a distinct idea of what kids you are looking for before the shoot?

A: At Parenting Magazine, we have a distinctive editorial style and our models reflect this. We try to choose real-looking kids, and kids who exude personality. We also use kids from all ethnic backgrounds to reflect the demographics of our ever-changing country.

Photo by Wilhelmina Models

Q: How do you go about booking kids?

A: Well, first of all, I'm in close contact with the modeling agencies. I rely on their years of expertise to inform me about who's who. They send me new composites and I also have go-sees.

Q: What does a go-see involve?

A: I inform the agencies that I'm having a casting for a shoot; they are usually open calls so hundreds of kids show up. We try to simulate a fashion shoot to get a sense of the child's personality. We take a snapshot of the children on the set to see how they behave away from their mothers and to get a feeling for them.

Q: After the go-see, what do you do?

A: We review our snapshots from the go-see, and book the kids when the clothes come in. We book through the agencies, giving them specifics such as date, time, location, and what the model should bring to the shoot, for example a favorite toy.

Q: What is a typical shoot like?

A: We book on a half-day basis to assure proper time to work with each child. I then select an outfit that picks up the child's unique personality and look. We always have a professional hair and

Photo by Michael Keel

makeup artist who does touch-ups to cover scrapes and to create some sort of whimsical hair style. Finally, the photographer works with the kids while I make sure the clothes and models look great.

Q: Sara, could you make any suggestions for parents who want their kids to succeed in modeling?

A: Parents should make sure that modeling is something the child wants to pursue. It involves a tremendous commitment from both the parent and the child and means missing some school. There are, however, enormous benefits to child modeling such as the financial rewards, and it teaches the kids to adapt to ever-changing circumstances, and to have self-confidence, discipline, and poise.

GENEVIEVE HERR, STYLIST

Genevieve is a hair and make-up artist in New York.

Q: What do you do?

A: I ask the client what kind of a look they want, and depending on that, you work with the kids. For the girls' hair, they will ask for curly or straight, accessories in the hair, etc.

Photo by Wilhelmina Models

Q: Do you use make-up for kids?

A: Usually very, very little. If the child is younger than 12, we usually don't apply any foundation unless the child has a scar or dark circles under the eyes—which is common with children—and then we apply just a little bit of concealer. Usually for girls I use blush, a little natural color on the lips, and maybe some mascara. If a boy has chapped lips or dry skin I will use moisturizer.

Q: How much time does it take to prepare a child for a shoot?

A: It takes about 15 minutes for the hair and 15 minutes for the make-up.

Q: How are kids to work with?

A: They're very easy to work with. They know the procedure, they sit still, and since they're not adults, they're not constantly on the phone while I'm trying to work!

Q: What is the role of the parent?

A: They usually sit in the make-up room with us. If the kid doesn't behave—which is rare—the parent can say something. Most of the kids are very well-behaved.

Photos by Wilhelmina Models

Q: Do you have any suggestions for parents taking their children to a go-see or a shoot?

A: The hair should be clean so that we can work with it. Teeth should be brushed and clean, and nails should be well-groomed.

Q: What clients have you worked with?

A: Capezio uses a lot of kids and I've worked with them often. I have also worked with children for Wrangler and Dupont and magazines including Child and Vogue.

JOANNE BLADES, FASHION STYLIST

Joanne is a fashion stylist in New York. She works with both adults and children.

Q: What do you do?

A: My job is basically to make sure that everyone looks good in what they are wearing. I mix and match the clothes that the client provides or that the models bring to the shoot, and sometimes I supply accessories to go with the clothing.

Photo by Wilhelmina Models

Q: How long does it take to do the styling for a child before a shoot?

A: It really depends on the age and manner of the child. Younger children take longer, especially very young ones, because you have to do everything for them. But older children can also take a long time because sometimes they won't like a particular outfit and will voice a strong opinion about it. You then have to take time to talk to them, because the models should like what they're wearing. They do a better job then.

It's hard to say how long it takes. At the beginning of the day it seems to take a long time, but as the day progresses and I get to know the models it becomes easier to work with them. For some models it becomes a game and they change very quickly!

Adults tend to understand that modeling is a business and it's their job to wear whatever they are given, but the kids don't always understand yet.

Q: What's it like to work with children in comparison to adults?

A: Most of the kids that I've worked with are a lot of fun. They're really cute, so it's a lot of fun for me and my assistant. The

Photo by Wilhelmina Models

atmosphere is really carefree. I worked on a Sahara Club catalog recently, which was shot on a rented farm, and we had the best time! There were five or six kids, and there were all sorts of things for them to do. There were ponies and other animals, and the kids just had a great time. In fact, most of the shoots that I've worked on with kids have been on location.

Q: Do you have any suggestions for parents before they bring their kids to a shoot?

A: Make sure that the kids have a good night of sleep and breakfast! Sometimes breakfast is provided at the shoot, but by the time the kids arrive they're so excited they forget to eat! In general, though, I've always had great experiences with kids.

Chapter 19
Glossary of Model Industry Terms

Photo by Jade Albert

AGENT
A person that represents talent in exchange for a commission of the talent's earnings.

AUDITION
A tryout for a part in a commercial or performance.

BOOK
To hire a model and schedule him or her for a shoot. This term is also used to refer to a model's portfolio.

CALL BACK
A request for a model to return for a second meeting with the casting director.

CASTING DIRECTOR
The person responsible for directing the selection of models for a shoot or commercial.

CATALOG HOUSE
A company responsible for the creation of catalogs for its clients.

CLIENT
A company or other entity that hires an agency to produce advertising, print work, or commercials.

Photo by Bob Cass

COMMERCIAL

A filmed advertisement shown on television.

COMMISSION

A percentage of a talent's gross earnings taken by an agent or manager in exchange for representation and other services.

COMPOSITE

Two or more pictures on an 8 X 10 sheet. Information such as height and weight may also be included.

CONTRACT

A legally binding agreement between two parties.

COPY

The written script for a commercial.

EDITORIAL SHOOT

Provides information; does not promote or advertise a product or service.

FASHION SHOOT

A shoot that shows new clothing styles or trends.

FLIPPER

A temporary denture or bridge used to fill in missing teeth in child models.

Photo by Bob Cass

GO-SEE
An audition for a modeling job.

HEADSHOT
An 8 X 10 photograph of the model's face.

INTERVIEW
A meeting between a model and a professional in order to secure a contract or job.

LOCAL MARKET
An area in which there are few major modeling and advertising agencies.

MAJOR MARKET
An area in which there are a multitude of modeling and advertising agencies and there is a strong demand for models. Includes New York, Los Angeles, Miami, and Chicago.

MANAGER
A person responsible for managing a model's career.

MARKETABILITY
The quality of being desired by agents and clients.

MODEL
A person who works as a subject for a photographer in order to display clothes or merchandise.

OFF SIZE
Sizes other than those in which clothing samples are produced.

OPEN CALL
A casting call that is open to anyone; models do not have to be sent through an agency.

PHOTOGENIC
The quality of photographing well.

PORTFOLIO
A collection of a model's photographs and examples of his or her work.

RESIDUALS
Payment for additional uses of an advertisement.

RESUME
A one-page summary of a model's statistics and experience. Information may include height, weight, eye and hair color, and previous work.

Alexander Cohen-Smith

D.O.B.: 4-1-87
Hair: Dark Blond
Eyes: Blue

Photos by Wilhelmina Models

SET
The location at which a shoot takes places. May be inside or outside.

SHOOT
A photography session.

STAGE PARENT
A parent who is overly concerned about his or her child's career.

TEARSHEET
An example of a model's work taken directly from a magazine or catalog.

TEST PHOTOGRAPHER
A photographer who takes photographs of new models for no charge or for a minimal charge.

TEST SHOT
A photograph of a new or aspiring model taken by a test photographer.

VOUCHER
A form that is used by a model to document the time of arrival and departure and rate of pay for a shoot.

WARDROBE
The collection of clothes owned by a model.

Appendix
National
Model Agency
Listing

ALASKA

AGENCY NAME	ADDRESS	CITY	STATE	ZIP	PHONE
John Robert Powers	300 E. Diamond Blvd, Suite B1	Anchorage	AK	99515	907-344-2525
Simply Pilar School Of Modeling	360 Boniface Parkway, A26	Anchorage	AK	99504	907-338-5736
Changes Unlimited	5259 Wright Lane	Fairbanks	AK	99712	907-452-2735
Critters of the Cinemat	44400 North Shaffer Rd.	Lake Hughes	AK	93532	800-233-3647

ALABAMA

Images	1212 Wilmer Ave.	Anniston	AL	36201	205-236-6335
Macy's School & Agency	20 1/2 E. 12th St.	Anniston	AL	36201	205-236-3597
The Agency	1212 Wilmer Ave.	Anniston	AL	36201	205-236-0952
Cathi Larsen Model & Talent	1628 6th St. N.W., Suite 205	Birmingham	AL	35215	205-871-2718
John Casablancas Center	3000 Riverchase Galleria 705	Birmingham	AL	35244	205-985-3001
Kiddin Around Models & Talent	700 S. 28th St., Suite 104	Birmingham	AL	35233	205-323-5437
Hamilton Acadamy	River Oaks Center, 1801 Beltline Rd.	Decatur	AL	35603	205-351-8022
PAMA Academy Model	1405 Weather Plz SE, Suite E	Huntsville	AL	35803	205-883-9992
Cynthia's Studio	3814 Harrison Rd.	Montgomery	AL	36109	205-272-5555
Shirley's Studio	503 N. Broadway	Sylacauga	AL	35150	205-245-2453
Naomi's Modeling School & Agency	P.O. Box 020198	Tuscaloosa	AL	35402-0198	205-345-1199

ARKANSAS

Agency	910 W. 6th St.	Little Rock	AR	72201	501-374-6447
Excel School of Modeling	8201 Cantrell Rd.	Little Rock	AR	72207	501-227-4232
Ferguson Modeling & Talent Agency	1100 W. 34th St.	Little Rock	AR	72206	501-375-3519
Glamour Modeling Agency	1105 North St.	Barling	AR	72923	501-452-3579

ARIZONA

Barbizon of Phoenix	1619A W. Bethany Home Rd.	Phoenix	AZ	85015	602-249-2950
Leighton Model & Talent Agency	3333 N. 44th St.	Phoenix	AZ	85018	602-224-9255
Tor/Ann Talent & Booking	6711 N. 21st Way	Phoenix	AZ	85016	602-263-8708
L'Image/John Casablancas	4533 N. Scottsdale Rd, Suite B	Scottsdale	AZ	85251	602-941-4838
Jean Fowler & Friends	10328 Cogins Dr. W.	Sun City	AZ	85351	602-977-8331
Robert Black Agency	20 E. University, Suite 206	Tempe	AZ	85281	602-966-2537
Signature	20 E. University, Suite 300	Tempe	AZ	85281	602-966-1102
ACT Theatrical & Modeling Agency	6264 E. Grant Rd.	Tucson	AZ	85712	602-885-3246
Flair	6700 N. Oracle Rd., #501	Tucson	AZ	85704	602-742-1090
Tom Thumb Agency	6902 E. Taos Pl.	Tucson	AZ	85715	602-885-3246

Medjuran Modeling Agency	1790 East River Rd.	Tuscon	AZ	85718	602-577-5143
Studio 5	1020 S. 4th Ave.	Yuma	AZ	85364	602-783-3666

CALIFORNIA

Norma Payton Henning	1361 Park St.	Alameda	CA	94501	510-523-7000
Barbizon Agency	2095 E. Ball Rd.	Anaheim	CA	92806	714-533-8100
Linda Fisher Modeling Agency	414 South Illinois	Anaheim	CA	92805	714-956-0815
Extrodinare Models & Talent	4437 Ming Ave.	Bakersfield	CA	93309	805-397-4440
McCright Agency	1011 Stine Rd.	Bakersfield	CA	93309	805-835-1305
Joan Mangum Agency	9250 Wilshire Blvd.	Beverly Hills	CA	90212	310-274-6622
Progressive Models	360 Mobile Ave., 102 A	Camarillo	CA	93010	805-484-5434
Elegance Modeling Studio & Talent Agency	2975 Madison St.	Carlsbad	CA	92008	619-434-3397
Clymer's Models &Talent Agency	7777 Greenback Lane	Citrus Heights	CA	95621	916-961-2144
The Model Center	151 Kalmus Dr., Suite J-1	Costa Mesa	CA	92626	714-662-1000
Dorie Model & Talent Agency	11750 Dublin Blvd., Suite 100	Dublin	CA	94568	415-551-7810
John Robert Powers	23710 E. 1 El Toro	El Toro	CA	92630	714-837-9900
Independent Model Network	1461 N Vanness Ave, Suite A	Fresno	CA	93728	209-233-9041
John Robert Powers	4747 N. First St., Suite 101	Fresno	CA	93710	209-244-6680
Your New Image	P.O. Box 33636	Grenada Hills	CA	91394	818-368-2036
Phyllis Cyr Modeling Academy	5872 Edinger Ave.	Huntington Beach	CA	92649	714-846-0215
Brand Model & Talent	17941 Sky Pk. Circle, Suite F	Irvine	CA	92714	714-251-0555
Beatrice Lilly Model & Talent Agency	1258 Prospect Ave.	La Jolla	CA	92037	619-454-3579
John Robert Powers	4443 Candlewood St.	Lakewood	CA	90712	213-531-2900
Barbizon Modeling School	3450 Wilshire Blvd, #90010	Los Angeles	CA	90004	213-487-1500
It Model Management	526 North larchmon	Los Angeles	CA	90038	213-962-5423
Nina Blanchard Agency	957 North Cole	Los Angeles	CA	90038	213-462-7274
Summer's Models of California	426 W. Main	Merced	CA	95340	204-383-3242
Platinum International Talent Agency	1050 N. Carpenter Rd., Suite 8	Modesto	CA	95351	209-578-1966
Rende Models Salon & Boutique	500 9th S., Suite K3	Modesto	CA	95354	209-526-6881
Artist Management	4340 Campus Dr., #210	Newport Beach	CA	92660	714-261-7557
Paul Gerard Talent Agency	2918 Alta Vista Dr.	Newport Beach	CA	92660	714-644-7950
Kids Hollywood	1151 Dove Street, #225	Newport Beach	CA	92660	714-851-0920
Models International	2103 El Camino Real, #101	Oceanside	CA	92054	619-433-6425
Elite School of Image	3509 E. Arderly Lane	Orange	CA	92667	714-998-2788
Cindy Romano School	P.O. Box 1951	Palm Springs	CA	92263	619-323-3333
Dorothy Shreve Agency	2665 N. Palm Cyn Dr.	Palm Springs	CA	92262	619-327-5855

Madlin's Modeling School & Agency	67-654 Ramon Rd.	Palm Springs	CA	92234	619-327-3060
Nouvelle Image Agency	200 Town & Country Village	Palo Alto	CA	94301	415-327-2757
Model & Talent Management	1610 Oak Park Blvd.	Pleasant Hill	CA	94523	510-932-4439
Academy of Arts	29 Massie Ct.	Sacramento	CA	95823	916-682-3362
Barbizon of Sacramento	701 Howe Ave., Suite H 50	Sacramento	CA	95825	916-920-4200
Ynobe International	9175 Kiefer Blvd.	Sacramento	CA	95826	916-362-6248
Model Perfect	1490 N. D St., Suite 1C	San Bernadino	CA	92405	909-880-2973
Barbizon School of Modeling	636 E. Brier Dr., Suite 150	San Bernardino	CA	92408	909-884-6266
Artist Management Agency	835 Fifth Ave., Suite 411	San Diego	CA	92101-6137	619-233-6655
Barbizon School of Modeling	591 Camino De La Reina	San Diego	CA	92108	619-296-6366
Janice Patterson Agency	2247 San Diego Ave #136	San Diego	CA	92110	619-295-9477
Neal Agency	3504 36th St.	San Diego	CA	92104	619-280-6910
Nouveau Model Management	9823 Pacific Hts Blvd, #M	San Diego	CA	92121	619-453-2727
San Diego Model Management	824 Camino Del Rio North, Suite 552	San Diego	CA	92108	619-296-1018
Shanon Freitas Model & Talent Agency	2400 Kettner Blvd., Suite #212	San Diego	CA	92101	619-621-2020
Tina Real Agency	3108 5th Ave., Suite C	San Diego	CA	92103	619-298-0544
Avalon Models	166 Geary St, Suite 1300	San Francisco	CA	94108	415-421-8211
City Model Management	123 Townsend St., Suite 510	San Francisco	CA	94107	410-546-3160
Film Theater Actors Exchange	582 Market St., Suite 302	San Francisco	CA	94133	415-433-3920
Grimme Agency	207 Powell St., 6th Floor	San Francisco	CA	94102	415-392-9175
John Robert Powers	30 Grant Ave., 3rd Floor	San Francisco	CA	94108	415-362-8260
Marla Dell Talent	1966 Union St., Suite 303	San Francisco	CA	94123	415-563-9213
Perseus Modeling & Talent	369 Pine St., Suite 500	San Francisco	CA	94104	415-391-1552
Quinn-Tonry Talent Agency	601 Brannan St.	San Francisco	CA	94107	415-543-3797
Stars Agency	777 Davis St.	San Francisco	CA	94111	415-421-6272
Barbizon of San Jose	3031 Tish Way, Suite 14	San Jose	CA	95128	408-247-2030
John Robert Powers	355 S. Daniel Way	San Jose	CA	95128	408-296-5100
Los Latinos Talent Agency	2801 Moorpark Ave., Suite 11	San Jose	CA	95128	408-296-2213
ACMT	265 South St., Suite F	San Luis Obispo	CA	93401	805-544-4500
Central Coast Model & Talent	265 South St., Suite F	San Luis Obispo	CA	93401	805-544-4500
J'Avance Agency	2901 W MacArthur Blvd., Suite 113	Santa Ana	CA	92704	714-979-8450
Susan Lane Model & Talent	14071 Windsor Pl.	Santa Ana	CA	92705	714-828-3643
Fontaine Talent Agency	20101 S.W. Birch St.	Santa Ana Hts	CA	92707	714-250-3018
Lorraine's International School Agency	1400 Glenn Canyon Rd.	Santa Cruz	CA	95060	408-425-7692
Covers Models & Talent Agency	2300 Bethards Dr.	Santa Rosa	CA	95405	707-575-5224

Julie Nation Acadamy	170 Farmers Lane	Santa Rosa	CA	95405	707-575-8585
Panda Talent Agency	3721 Hoen Ave.	Santa Rosa	CA	94505	707-576-0711
John Robert Powers	15301 Ventura Blvd., Suite 305	Sherman Oaks	CA	91403	818-789-7146
Charm	1456 W. Mendocino Ave.	Stockton	CA	95204	209-464-3708
Malone's Model Management	1249 Stratford Circle, P.O. Box 7820	Stockton	CA	95207	209-473-7153
Studio One Models Agency & Training	7233 Pacific Ave.	Stockton	CA	95207	209-931-3606
John Robert Powers	23825 Hawthorne Blvd.	Torrance	CA	90505	310-378-0767
Stafford School of Charm	114 W. Main St., Suite 20	Visalia	CA	93277	209-734-3445
Hollywood Film School	2500 Suite K Towngate	Westlake Village	CA	91361	805-496-9716
John Robert Powers	16434 Beach Blvd.	Westminister	CA	92683	714-375-4400

COLORADO

John Robert Powers	14231 E. 4th Ave., Suite 200	Aurora	CO	80010	303-340-2838
MTA	1026 W. Colorado Ave.	Colorado Spgs	CO	80904	719-577-4704
Jeanines Modeling & Talent Agency	1227 Mt. View	Colorado Springs	CO	80907	719-598-4507
Barbizon Agency of Denver	7535 E. Hampden Ave.	Denver	CO	80231	303-337-7954
Europa	1430 Larimer St., Suite 206	Denver	CO	80202	303-446-0445
Europa International Model Agency	1430 Larimar St./Larimar Sq., Ste 206	Denver	CO	80202	303-446-0445
John Casablancas	7600 E Eastman Ave., Suite 100	Denver	CO	80231	303-337-5100
Leiten Agency	1514 Blake St.	Denver	CO	80202	303-893-3339
Maximum Talent	3900 E. Mexico Ave., Suite 105	Denver	CO	80210	303-691-2344
TX Talents	1660 17th St., Suite 101	Denver	CO	80202	303-623-7274
Kids Kits	601 S. Broadway, Suite F	Denver	CO	80209	303-733-2852
Silhouettes Talent Agency	7717 W. 6th Ave.	Lakewood	CO	80215	303-333-1360
JF Talent	5161 E Arapahoe Rd., Suite 400	Littleton	CO	80121	303-779-8888

CONNECTICUT

Show Biz Kids	700 W. Johnson Ave.	Chesire	CT	06410	203-250-8268
Barbizon School & Agency	2969 Whitney Ave., Suite 202	Hamdon	CT	06518	203-248-6633
John Casablancas Model & Talent Management	461 Farmington Ave.	Hartford	CT	06105	203-232-4421
Johnston Agency	50 Washington St.	South Norwalk	CT	06854	203-838-6188
Barbizon School	26 6th St.	Stamford	CT	06905	203-248-6633
Creative Talent	P.O. Box 143	E. Glastonbury	CT	06025	203-295-1060
World Promotions	250 Sargent Dr.	New Haven	CT	6511	203-781-3427
Joanna Lawrence Agency	82 Patrick Road	Westport	CT	06880	203-226-7239

John Casablancas Model & Talent Management	214 Amity Road	Woodbridge	CT	06525	203-397-3570
Jaguar Agency	140 Capt. Thos Blvd.	West Haven	CT	06516	203-932-0744

DISTRICT OF C 1BIA

Central Casting	623 Pennsylvania Ave. S.E.	Washington	DC	20003	410-889-3200
Jump Studio	3333 K St. N.W.	Washington	DC	20007	202-333-2280
Mich Royal Model & Talent	P.O. Box 5168	Washington	DC	20091-1068	202-466-2066
Anne Schwabb's Model Store	1529 Wisconsin Ave. N.W.	Washington	DC	20007	202-333-3560
Precola's Beauty Image	901 6th St. S.W. Ave.	Washington	DC	20024	202-484-9300
T.H.E. Artist Agency	3068 M St. N.W.	Georgetown	DC	20007	202-342-0933

DELAWARE

Barbizon Modeling School	17B Trolley Square, Suite 7B	Wilmington	DE	19806	302-658-6666
Dupont Model Management	3422 Old Capitol Trail	Wilmington	DE	19808	302-774-1000

FLORIDA

June 2 Models	249 W. State Road 436, Suite 1101	Altamonte Springs	FL	32714	407-869-1144
Barbizon of Orlando	280 S. State Road. 434, Suite 2042	Altamonte Springs	FL	32714	407-774-3110
John Robert Powers	1052 W. State Road, Suite 2062	Altamonte Springs	FL	32714	407-774-7616
Ashley Simonson Models	One Camino Real, Suite 101	Boca Raton	FL	33432	407-367-0000
Barbizon International	1900 Glades Rd., Suite 300	Boca Raton	FL	33431	407-362-8883
Studio Model	5499 North Federal Highway	Boca Raton	FL	33487	407-995-8727
Ellen Meade Studios	1323 63rd Ave. E.	Bradenton	FL	34203	813-755-1757
Allstare Models & Talent	30 Cotillion Ct.	Casselberry	FL	32707	407-339-3612
Hamilton-Hall Talent Agency	13700 58th St. N., Suite 201	Clearwater	FL	34620	813-538-3838
Beauty Works	3390 Mary St.	Cocoanut Grove	FL	33133	305-446-6892
Model Development	3390 Mary St. PH-D	Cocoanut Grove	FL	33133	305-447-1113
Gabriel Models	2115 Lejuene Rd.	Coral Gables	FL	33134	305-444-1999
Boca Talent	829 S.E. 9th St.	Deerfield	FL	33441	305-428-4677
A-1 Pegs Model & Talent Agency	133 E. Lauren Ct.	Fern Pk	FL	32730	407-834-0406
Central Casting of Florida	411 N.E. 11th Ave.	Ft. Lauderdale	FL	33301	305-525-8351
John Casablancas Center	3343 W Comm'l Blvd., Suite 106	Ft. Lauderdale	FL	33306	305-731-6333
John Robert Powers of Ft. Lauderdale	828 S.E. 4th St.	Ft. Lauderdale	FL	33301	305-467-2838
Models Exchange	2425 E. Commercial Blvd., Suite 206	Ft. Lauderdale	FL	33308	305-491-1014
Scott Harvey Model & Talent Agency	2734 E. Oakland Park Blvd., Suite 107	Ft. Lauderdale	FL	33306	305-565-1211
Firestone Model & Talent Agency	31 Barkley Circle, Suite 1	Ft. Myers	FL	33907	813-939-3880
Dawn Doyle Agency	828 S.E. 4th St.	Ft. Lauderdale	FL	33301	305-467-2838

Longshot Talent Agency	1483 Southern Drive S.W.	Ft. Myers	Fl	33919	813-433-0248
Just Faces	P.O. Box 12552	Ft. Pierce	FL	34949	
Modeling Connection	6787 Newberyy Rd.	Gainsville	FL	32605	904-331-0205
Miami Talent Agency	Plantation Executive Building, 278 South University Dr.	Hollywood	FL	33324	305-472-1717
Brevard Talent Group	405 Palm Springs Blvd.	Indian Harbor Beach	FL	32937	407-773-1355
MDM Studios-Acting-Modeling School	968 Pinetree Dr.	Indian Harbor Beach	FL	32937	407-777-1344
Denise Carol Models & Talent	3236 Beach Blvd.	Jacksonville	FL	32207	904-399-0824
ACT I	1220 Collins Ave.	Miami	FL	33139	305-672-0200
Barbizon School & Agency	782 N.W. Lejune Rd., Suite 333	Miami	FL	33126	305-437-7900
Beauty Search Models & Pageant	420 Lincoln Rd.	Miami	FL	33143	305-532-4147
Creative Arts Time	7540 S.W. 59 Ct.	Miami	FL	33143	305-667-8773
Int'l Models	7951 S.W. Bird Rd., Suite 211	Miami	FL	33155	305-266-6331
John Casablancas Center	10491 N. Kendall Dr.	Miami	FL	33176	305-596-7107
Next Models	209 Ninth St.	Miami	FL	33139	305-531-5100
Runways	9350 S. Dixie Hwy., Penthouse 3	Miami	FL	33156	305-670-3003
Ellen Jacoby Casting	420 Lincoln Rd., Suite 210	Miami Beach	FL	33139	305-531-5300
Ford Models	800 Ocean Dr.	Miami Beach	FL	33139	305-534-7200
Irene Marie	728 Ocean Dr.	Miami Beach	FL	33139	305-672-2929
L'Agence Models	1220 Collins Ave.	Miami Beach	FL	33139	305-672-0804
Modele by Bobbi Kemp	420 Lincoln Rd., Suite 331	Miami Beach	FL	33139	305-534-7701
Stellar Talent / Agency	1234 Washington Ave.	Miami Beach	FL	33139	305-672-2217
Travis Falcon Agency	17070 Collins Ave., Suite 231	Miami Beach	FL	33160	305-947-7957
Charmette Modeling Agency	500 Deer Run Dr.	Miami Springs	FL	33166	305-871-8253
Ada Gordon Talent	1995 NE 150th St., Suite C	N Miami	FL	33181	305-940-1311
Green & Green Model & Talent Agency	12550 Biscayne Blvd., Suite 403	N Miami	FL	33181	305-674-9900
The Modeling Connection & Rasberry	2248 N. Tamiami T	Naples	FL	33940	813-262-6607
Mary Lou's Model Management International	P.O. Box 5127	Navarre	FL	32566	904-932-7330
Marbea Agency	1946 N.E. 149th St.	North Miami Beach	FL	33181	305-964-7401
Anne O'Briant Agency	2811 Marsala Ct.	Orlando	FL	32806	407-649-9841
Dimensions III	5205 S. Orange Ave.	Orlando	FL	32809	407-851-2575
Model Consultant	3300 Haviland Ct., Suite 303	Palm Harbor	FL	34684	813-786-1664
First Impressions Modeling Association	4699 N. Fed'l Hwy.	Pompano Beach	FL	33064	305-785-7998
Suzi's International Models	2426 Bee Ridge Rd.	Sarasota	FL	34231	813-922-5339
Valkert Career Center	7551 Calle Facil	Sarasota	FL	34238	813-925-8660

Stephanie Gibbs Model & Talent	1365-D South Patrick Dr.	Satellite Beach	FL	32937	407-777-9127
Smarter Images	2195 Ocean Blvd.	Stuart	FL	34994	407-288-1188
Turnabout Talent Agencies	584 SE Monterey Rd.	Stuart	FL	34994	407-283-1449
Marsha Model of the South	4130 East Bugie View	Talahassee	FL	32311	904-656-2600
Set Five Models & Talent	714 Glenview Dr.	Tallahassee	FL	32303	904-224-8500
Studio Elle	P.O. Box 559	Tallevast	FL	34270	813-351-1599
Avance Model & Talent Agency	406 N. Reo St., Suite 239	Tampa	FL	33609	813-289-9816
Barbizon School of Modeling	4600 W. Cypress St., Suite 410	Tampa	FL	33607	813-286-9999
Dorsett Models	16057 Tampa Palms Blvd W., Regency Suite 264	Tampa	FL	33647-2001	813-977-5096
Evelyn Stewart's Modeling & Talent	12421 N. Florida Ave., Suite D218	Tampa	FL	33612	813-935-2208
First Impressions Image & Modeling	41 Davis Blvd.	Tampa	FL	33606	813-251-1008
Independent Castings	8313 W Hillsborough Ave., Suite 4	Tampa	FL	33615	813-884-8335
Irene Marie	1413 S. Howard, Suite 101	Tampa	FL	33606	813-251-5221
John Cassablanca	5215 W Laurel St., Suite 203	Tampa	FL	33607	813-289-8564
Model Limited Agency	6717 Hanley Rd.	Tampa	FL	33614	813-885-6609
Tampa Bay Talent	5215 W Laurel St., Suite 203	Tampa	FL	33607	813-264-6448
Looking Glass	5217 Michael Dr., Suite 201	Temple Terrace	FL	33617	
Fashion Mystique Modeling Agency	P.O. Box 1288	Umatilla	FL	32784	
Turnabout Talent Agencies	1630 Club Dr.	Vero Beach	FL	32963	407-231-4579
Sarah Parker	1696 Old Okee Chobee, Studio 1C	West Palm Beach	FL	33409	407-686-7201
Montage Models & Talent	1165 1st St. S.	Winter Haven	FL	33880	813-293-5363
Azuree Model & Talent Agency	140 N. Orlando Ave., Suite 120	Winter Park	FL	32789	407-629-5025
Lisa Maile School	999 S. Orlando Ave.	Winter Park	FL	32789	407-628-5989
Modelscout Inc.	507 N. New York Ave., Rail Road Car 2	Winter Park	FL	32789	407-645-1466
Susanne Haley Talent	618 Wymore Rd., Suite 2	Winter Park	FL	32789	407-644-0600
Christensen Group	P.O. Box 2396	Winter Park	FL	32790	407-628-8803
Hurt-Garver Talent	400 N. New York Ave., Suite 207	Winter Park	FL	32789	407-740-5700
Images & Modeling/Lisa Maile School	999 South Orlando Ave.	Winter Park	FL	32789	407-628-5989
John Casablancas Center	329 Park Ave. S., Suite 200	Winter Park	FL	32789	407-740-6697

GEORGIA

Michele's Models	1100 Breckenridge Dr.	Adel	GA	31620	912-896-4490
Millie Lewis	2615 Gillionville Rd., Suite 4	Albany	GA	31707	912-432-9368
Donna Summers Talent	8950 Laurel Way	Alpharetta	GA	30202	404-518-9855
Athens Modeling	114 -D South Park Ave.	Athens	GA	32789	706-546-8831

Ah! Annie Harvey Talent	77 E Andrews Dr., Suite 243	Atlanta	GA	30305	404-266-0427
Arlene Wilson Model Management	887 W Marietta St. N.W., Suite N101	Atlanta	GA	30318	404-876-8555
Atlanta Models & Talent	3030 Peachtree Rd. N.W.	Atlanta	GA	30305	404-261-9627
Atlanta's Young Faces	6075 Roswell Rd. N.E., Suite 118	Atlanta	GA	30328	404-255-3080
ATP Casting	2956 Hardman Ct.	Atlanta	GA	30305	404-233-2278
Barbizon of Atlanta	3340 Peachtree Rd. N.E., Suite 120	Atlanta	GA	30326	404-261-7332
Burns Agency	3210 Peachtree Rd. N.E., Suite 9	Atlanta	GA	30305	404-299-8114
Chadz Model Management/IFS	3166 Maple Dr., Suite 221	Atlanta	GA	30339	404-261-4989
Chez Casting	572 Armour Circle N.E.	Atlanta	GA	30324	404-873-1215
Elite Model Management	181 14th St., Suite 325	Atlanta	GA	30309	404-872-7444
Fash Institute of Atlanta	3376 Peachtree Rd. N.E.	Atlanta	GA	30326	404-266-2662
Fashion Office	250 Spring St. N.W., Suite 25337	Atlanta	GA	30303	404-220-2833
Glynn Kennedy	133 Carnegie N.W., Suite 200	Atlanta	GA	30305	404-892-5500
John Casablancas Center	4501 Circle 75 Pkwy., Suite F6180	Atlanta	GA	30339	404-951-9564
L'Agence	5901 Peachtree Dunwoody Rd. N.E., Suite 60	Atlanta	GA	30328	404-396-9015
People's Store	1776 Peachtree Rd. N.W., Suite 336 South	Atlanta	GA	30309	404-874-6448
Serendity Models International	550 Pharr Rd. N.E., Suite 220	Atlanta	GA	30305	404-237-4040
Stilwell Casting	2956 Hardman Ct.	Atlanta	GA	30305	404-233-2278
TMA-Talent Management of Atlanta	1702 Dunwoody Pl.	Atlanta	GA	30324	404-231-1778
Advance Agency Model & Talent Center	418 Bradley St.	Carrolton	GA	30117	404-834-9972
Mable Bailey Fashion College	3115 Cross County Hill	Columbus	GA	31906	706-563-0606
Mademoiselles-Leebern Agency	3617 Hilton Ave., Suite 212	Columbus	GA	31904	706-327-4636
Merchant Models	1018 North Glenwood	Dalton	GA	30721	706-278-4639
Cynthia Johnson	P.O. Box 3330	Ft Stewart	GA	31314	912-876-8679
Elaine Barthe	6500 McDonough Dr., Suite E1	Norcrossa	GA	30093	404-476-5085
Studio Model Management	5430 Jimmy Carter Blvd., Suite 212	Norcrossa	GA	30093	404-729-8511
Lorren & Macy's Acadamy	405 1/2 Broad St.	Rome	GA	30161	706-235-1175
Millie Lewis Models	7011 Hodson Memorial Dr.	Savannah	GA	31406	912-354-9525
Mary Owens Charm & Fashion School	223 N. Central Ave.	Tifton	GA	31794	912-386-0676
Sylvia School of Modeling	1011 Williams St.	Valdosta	GA	31601	912-244-9275

HAWAII

JJ Productions	98-021 Kam Hwy., 2nd Floor	Aiea, Oahu	HI	96701	808-486-1656
ADR Productions	431 Kuwili St.	Honolulu	HI	96817	808-524-4777
Barbizon School of Modeling	1600 Kapiolani Blvd., Suite 1230	Honolulu	HI	96814	808-946-9081

John Robert Powers	1314 South King St., Suite 504	Honolulu	HI	96814	808-521-4908
Kathy Muller Talent & Modeling Agency	619 Kapahulu Ave., Penthouse	Honolulu	HI	96815	808-737-7917
Kotomori Agency	1018 Hoawa Ln.	Honolulu	HI	96826	808-955-6511
LA Image	1050 Ala Moana Blvd.	Honolulu	HI	96817	808-591-0588
Leslie Ringe Produces	950 Ahuvale Pl.	Honolulu	HI	96821	808-377-1110
MWM Production Agency	229 Paoakalani Ave., Suite 600	Honolulu	HI	96815	808-945-7809
Ruth Woodhall Talent Agency	2003 Kalia Rd., Suite 12F	Honolulu	HI	96815	808-947-3307
Sohbi Talent Agency	1750 Kalakau Ave., Suite 116	Honolulu	HI	96826	808-946-6614
SOS Hawaii/Lani Petranek	1519 Nuuanu Ave., KT 41	Honolulu	HI	96817	808-524-7478
Susan Page's Modeling & Talent	1441 Kapiolani Blvd., Suite 1220	Honolulu	HI	96814	808-955-2271
Island Faces	1024 Kamalu Rd.	Kapaa	HI	96746	808-822-7623
Central Island Agency/CIA Models Hawaii	41-846 Lausilo St.	Waimanalo	HI	96795	808-259-7914

IOWA

ADA Gaffney Shaff	#1 Cumberland Corners, 2828 18th Street	Bettendorf	IA	52722	319-359-6144
Corrine Shover Model School & Agency	4646 First Ave. N.E.	Cedar Rapids	IA	52402	319-395-7772
Avant Studios	7600 University, Suite D	Des Moines	IA	50325	515-255-0297
The Agency, Faces & Talent	246 Wilson Ave. S.W.	Cedar Rapids	IA	52402	319-366-3951
Elan Training & Talent	223 Lenora Dr. N.W.	Cedar Rapids	IA	52405	319-396-5666

IDAHO

Blanche B. Evans Models Management & Agency	205 N. Tenth, Suite 500	Boise	ID	83702	208-344-5380
Metcalf Models	1851 Century Way, Suite 3	Boise	ID	83709	208-378-8777
Images	132 N. Woodruff, Suite J	Idaho Falls	ID	83401	208-529-3771
Fashion Faces Modeling	2946 S. Frontage Rd.	American Falls	ID	83211	208-232-6574

ILLINOIS

Patricia Ray Modeling School	975 Aurora Ave.	Aurora	IL	60505	708-859-3444
Glamour Models	P.O. Box 275	Charleston	IL	61920	217-348-1211
Allied Artists Agency	811 W. Evergreen	Chicago	IL	60622	312-482-8488
Ambassador Talents	203 N. Wabash Ave., Suite 220	Chicago	IL	60601	312-641-3491
Aria Model & Talent Management	1017 W. Washington, Suite 2A	Chicago	IL	60607	312-243-9400
Arlene Wilson Model Management	430 W. Erie St., Suite 210	Chicago	IL	60610	312-573-0200
Barbizon	303 E. Ohio	Chicago	Il	60611	312-329-9405
Barbizon Agency of Chicago	541 N. Fairbanks	Chicago	IL	60611	312-329-9405
Chicago Model & Talent Management	435 N. La Salle St.	Chicago	IL	60610	312-527-2977

Elite Model Management	212 W. Superior St., Suite 406	Chicago	IL	60610	312-943-3226
Emila Lorence	619 N. Wabash	Chicago	IL	60611	312-787-2033
ETA	7588 S. Chicago Ave.	Chicago	IL	60619	312-752-3955
Geddes Agency	1925 N. Clybourn Ave., Suite 402	Chicago	IL	60614	312-348-3333
Jefferson & Associates	1050 N. State St.	Chicago	Il	60610	312-337-1930
John Casablancas Modeling & Career Center	435 N. La Salle St., Suite 100	Chicago	IL	60610	312-670-2113
John Robert Powers School	27 E. Monroe St., Room 200	Chicago	IL	60603	312-726-1404
Knutsen Casting	919 N. Michigan Ave., Suite 3011	Chicago	IL	60611	312-649-1167
Lily's Talent Agency	5962 N. Elston	Chicago	IL	60646	312-792-1366
North Shore Model & Talent	308 W. Erie, Suite 310	Chicago	IL	60610	312-482-9949
Nouvelle Talent Management	P.O. Box 578100	Chicago	IL	60657-8100	312-944-1133
Phoenix Talent	410 South Michigan, Penthouse Suite	Chicago	IL	60605	312-786-2024
Salazar & Navas	367 W. Chicago Ave., Suite 200	Chicago	IL	60610	312-751-3419
Shirley Hasilton	333 E. Ontairo, Suite B	Chicago	IL	60611	312-787-4700
Stewart Talent Management Corporation	212 W. Superior, Suite 406	Chicago	IL	60610	312-943-0892
Susanne's A-Plus	108 W. Oak St.	Chicago	IL	60610	312-943-8315
Larry Bastian	2580 Crestwood Ln.	Deerfield	IL	60015	708-945-9283
Norman Schucart Entertainment	1417 Green Bay Rd.	Highland Pk.	IL	60035	708-433-1113
Lisa's School of Modeling	200 North 8th St.	Quincy	IL	62306	217-224-4052
Barbizon School of Schaumburg	600 Woodfield Dr.	Schaumburg	IL	60172	308-240-4200
Royal Model Management	1051 Perimeter Dr.	Schaumburg	IL	60173	708-240-4215
AWA Productions	37 Oakmont Dr.	Springfield	IL	62704	217-546-4825
Dance Arts	2820 S MacArthur	Springfield	IL	62704	217-522-9064
John Casablancas	Danata Square E., Suite 39	Wheaton	IL	60187	708-260-0808
Harrise Davidson Talent Agency	65 E.Wacker Pl., Suite 2401	Chicago	IL	60601	312-782-4480

INDIANA

Helen Wells Agency	1711 N. Meridian St., Suite 640	Carmel	IN	46032	317-843-5363
Super Models	14420 Cherry Tree Lane	Carmel	IN	46033	317-846-4321
Beau Madame School & Agency	1324 N. Green River Rd.	Evansville	IN	47715-2427	812-476-4800
Evelyn Lahaie School	P.O. Box 614	Hobart	IN	46342	219-942-4670
Scalina & Brown Model Development	6285 N. College Ave., Suite 1	Indianapolis	IN	46220	317-848-4026
Super Models International	6330 E. 75th St., Suite 300	Indianapolis	IN	46250	317-846-4321
Models' Registry	423 E. Lincoln Rd.	Kokomo	IN	46902	317-453-5170
AAA Modeling Agency	736 E. 10th Pl.	Mishamaka	IN	46544	219-255-7275
CJ Mercury	1330 Lake Ave.	Whiting	IN	46394	219-659-2701

Charmaine School & Model Agency	3538 Stellhorn Rd.	Fort Wayne	IN	46815	219-485-8421

KANSAS

Career Images Model & Talent Agency	8519 Lathrop Ave.	Kansas City	KS	66109	913-334-2200
The Agency, Models & Talent	4711 Lamar Ave.	Mission	KS	66202	913-362-8382
Hoffman International	10540 Marty, Suite 100	Overland Park	KS	66212	913-642-1060
J Miller & Summer Agency	10928 W. 74th St.	Shawnee	KS	66203	913-631-6113
Models & Images	1619 N. Rock Rd., Suite E	Wichita	KS	67206	316-674-2777
JW Prods	2414 N. Woodlawn	Wichita	KS	67220	316-686-5336
Model Connection	P.O. Box 1304	Mission	KS	66222	816-753-0166

KENTUCKY

Alix Adams Agency	9813 Merioneth Dr.	Jeffersontown	KY	40299	502-266-6990
Images Model Agency	163 E. Reynolds Dr.	Lexington	KY	40517	606-273-2301
Vogue of Lexington Model & Talent Agency	1300 N.E. New Circle Rd.	Lexington	KY	40555	606-254-4582
Cosmo Modeling Agency	7410 LaGrange Rd., Suite 204	Louisville	KY	40222	502-425-8000
Vogue Modeling	2027 Frankfort Ave.	Louisville	KY	40206	502-897-0089
Uptown Images	223 S. Main St.	Harrodsburg	KY	40330	606-734-4394

LOUISIANA

Dolly Dean for Talent	3617 S. Sherwood Forest Blvd., Suite B	Baton Rouge	LA	70816	504-292-2424
Don Clark For Talent	P.O. Box 248	Baton Rouge	LA	70851	504-272-1927
Ibelco Modeling School	1986 Dallas Dr., Suite 13	Baton Rouge	LA	70806	504-924-4852
Faces Modeling of Louisana	P.O. Box 92243	Lafayette	LA	70509	318-235-3223
Images	1 Flag Place, Suites 3 & 4	Lafayette	LA	70508	318-984-9841
Through the Looking Glass	1090 Entrance Rd.	Leesville	LA	71446	318-537-5733
Faces Model Management	2637 Edenborn Ave., Suite 6	Metarie	LA	70002	504-455-9959
MTP	One Galleria Blvd., Suite 825	Metarie	LA	70000	504-831-8000
The Agency	P.O. Box 714	Metarie	LA	70004	504-288-8085
Sass Agency	P.O. Box 13544	New Iberia	LA	70562-3544	
Del Corral Agency	101 W. Robert E. Lee Blvd., Suite 205	New Orleans	LA	70124	504-288-8963
Fame Model & Talent Agency	1725 Caronoelet St.	New Orleans	LA	70130	504-522-2001
New Orleans Model & Talent Agency	1347 Magazine St.	New Orleans	LA	70130	504-525-0100
Mister Lynn's	2746 Mackey Lane	Shreveport	LA	71118	318-687-8922

MASSACHUSETTS

La Femmina #4	862 Brockton Ave.	Abington	MA	02351	617-878-4390
Cameo Kids	437 Boylston St.	Boston	MA	02116	617-536-6004

Chute Agency	115 Newbury St.	Boston	MA	02116	617-262-2626
Copley Seven	P.O. Box 535	Boston	MA	02117	617-267-4444
Folio Models	25 Huntington Ave., Suite 500	Boston	MA	02116	617-267-0240
John Robert Powers	9 Newbury St.	Boston	MA	02116	617-267-8781
Lordly & Dame	51 Church St.	Boston	MA	02116	617-482-3593
Maggie	35 Newbury St.	Boston	MA	02116	617-536-2639
Model Club	229 Berkley St.	Boston	MA	02116	617-247-9020
Models Group	374 Congress St., Suite 305	Boston	MA	02110	617-426-4711
Models Inc.	218 Newbury St.	Boston	MA	02116	617-437-6212
Viva International	25 Huntington Ave.	Boston	MA	02116	617-266-0880
Loretta Davis Modeling Agency	965 Concord St.	Framingham	MA	01701	508-872-6039
La Femmina	46 Pearl St.	Hyannis	MA	02601	508-778-1557
Finishing Touch	46 Alcoh St.	Lowell	MA	01852	508-458-4410
Cinderella Modeling Studio & Agency	65 Clinton St.	Malden	MA	02148	617-324-7590
La Femmina Modeling School	145 Faunce Corner Rd.	North Dartmouth	MA	02747	508-999-4424
Prestige Ave. Models	195 Worthington St.	Springfield	MA	01103	413-733-1770
John Robert Powers	390 Main St.	Worcester	MA	01608	508-753-6343
La Femminina Models	3-15 East Mountain St.	Worcester	MA	01606	508-852-0444

MARYLAND

Chris Barry Talent Consultant	205 E. Joppa Road	Baltimore	MD	21286	410-321-1611
King Prods & Talent Agency	8900 Edgeworth Dr., Suite B	Capital Heights	MD	20743	301-350-9778
Ann Carter Studios	1697 Barrister Ct.	Crofton	MD	21114	410-793-3853
Marmo-Willett Prods	3 Trudy Way	Gaithersburg	MD	20878	301-924-5016
Annapolis Agency/Shaw Studio	500A Ritchey Hwy	Severna Park	MD	21146	410-6471200
MTM/John Casablancas Agency	7801 York Road	Towson	MD	21204	410-821-6966
Barbizon Model Agency	12250 Rockville Pike, Suite 230	Rockville	MD	20852	301-770-0606

MAINE

Gibson Girl Modeling & Casting	650 Forest Ave.	Portland	ME	04101	207-772-2638
Portland Models Group	7 Oak Hill Terrace	Scarborough	ME	04074	207-885-5793

MICHIGAN

Michael Jeffrey's Model/Talent Agency	122 S. Main St., Suite 270	Ann Arbor	MI	48104	313-663-6398
Production Plus	30600 Telegraph Rd., Suite 2181	Birmingham	MI	48110	313-644-5566
Talent Shop	30100 Telegraph Rd.	Birmingham	MI	48025	313-644-4877
Tiffany's International Modeling & Talent	159 S. Broadway, Suite 116	Cassoplis	MI	49031	616-445-8346

Kross Talent	1993 East Intermediate	Central Lake	MI	49622	616-544-9860
Advantage-Model Consultant	4321 Bluebird	Commerce Twp	MI	48382	313-363-5500
Maxine Powell School	8106 E. Jefferson Blvd., Suite 209	Detroit	MI	48208	313-331-4333
Promotional United Modeling and Referral Service	12620 Washburn	Detroit	MI	48238	
Wayman Talent Agency	1959 Jefferson, Suite 4H	Detroit	MI	48207	313-393-8300
Avante Modeling Agency	3426 Miller Rd., Suite C100	Flint	MI	48507	313-732-2233
Cynthianna Models and Talent	P.O. Box 667	Flushimg	MI	48433	313-659-5996
Robert Brooks Fashion & Modeling Center	32605 W. Twelve Mile Road	Farmington Hills	MI	48334	
Pastiche Model & Talent	200 E. Bldg, 1514 Wealthy St. S.E., Suite 280	Grand Rapids	MI	49505	616-451-2181
Uniquely You Model & Talent Agency	4485 Plainfield N.E., Suite 102	Grand Rapids	MI	49505	606-365-0959
Adam's Pro Modeling & Finishing School	1625 Haslett Rd.	Haslett	MI	48840	517-339-9061
John Casablancas Modeling & Career	44450 Pinetree Dr.	Plymouth	MI	48170	313-455-0700
Models International & Talent Agency	713 Ashmund St., Suite 201	Saulste. Marie	MI	49783	906-632-6411
Gail & Rice Productions	24660 Lanser	Southfield	MI	48034	313-799-5053
John Robert Powers	16250 N'land Dr., Suite 239	Southfield	MI	48075	313-569-1234
Milane Model Management	29425 N.W. Hwy., Suite 100	Southfield	MI	40834	313-358-1125
Affiliated Models	1680 Crooks Rd.	Troy	MI	48840	313-244-8770
John Casablancas Modeling & Career	1197 E. Big River Rd., The Affliated Building	Troy	MI	48083	313-689-1090
Barbizon Of Modeling	6230 Orchard Lake Rd.	W. Bloomfield	MI	48322	213-855-5660
Nique's Model Tique	954 Ecorse Rd.	Ypsilanti	MI	48198	313-483-7161

MINNESOTA

Deephaven School of Modeling & Acting	18178 Minnnetonka Blvd.	Deephaven	MN	55391	612-449-9992
John Casablancas Center	7701 South York, Suite 370	Edina	MN	55435	612-825-5512
Kimberly Franson Agency	4620 W. 77th St., Suite 209	Edina	MN	55435	612-830-0111
John Casablancas Center	2785 White Bear Ave., Suite 108	Maplewood	MN	55104	612-777-5660
Caryn School of Modeling	63 S. Ninth St., Suite 200	Minneapolis	MN	55402	612-338-0102
Creative Casting	10 S. Fifth St., Suite 860	Minneapolis	MN	55402-1010	612-375-0525
Elenor Moore Agency	1610 W. Lake St.	Minneapolis	MN	55408	612-827-3823
Models Resource Center	27 N. 4th St., Suite 202	Minneapolis	MN	55401	612-339-2441
New Faces	5217 Wayzata Blvd., Suite 210	Minneapolis	MN	55416	612-544-8668
Paramount Modeling & Talent	126 North 3rd St., Suite 502	Minneapolis	MN	55401	612-333-3536
Plaza 3 Talent & Model Agency	15 S. Fifth St.	Minneapolis	MN	55402	612-338-5900
Scott Winnick Agency	5445 Newton Ave. S., Suite 200	Minneapolis	MN	55419	612-920-1106

Wehmann Model & Talent	1128 Harmon Pl., Suite 205	Minneapolis	MN	55403	612-333-6393

MISSOURI

Barbizon School	7525 Forsyth Ave.	Clayton	MO	63105-3499	314-863-1141
Prima Models	522A South Hanley	Clayton	MO	63105	314-436-7705
Images of St Louis	715 Old Frontenac Sq.	Frontenac	MO	63131	314-993-0605
John Robert Powers	711 Old Frontenac Sq.	Frontenac	MO	63131	314-993-3097
The Models & Talent Network	123 1/2 W. Lexington	Independence	MO	64050	816-252-4368
John Casablancas Center	330 West 47th St., Suite 220	Kansas City	MO	64112	816-561-9400
MTC Model Talent Charm	4043 Broadway	Kansas City	MO	64111	816-531-3223
Patricia Stevens Model Agency	4638 JC Nichols Pkwy	Kansas City	MO	64112	816-531-3800
Professional Edge	P.O. Box 841	Kirksville	MO	63501	816-665-2464
Delcia Agency	7201 Delamr Ave.	St. Louis	MO	63130	314-947-0120
John Casablancas Center	11815 Manchester Rd.	St. Louis	MO	63131	314-965-9001
Model Management	11815 Manchester Rd.	St. Louis	MO	63131	314-965-3264
Talent Plus	55 Maryland Plaza	St. Louis	MO	63108	314-367-5588
Talent Source	14 S. Euclid Suite D	St. Louis	MO	63108	314-367-8585
Kids Pix Agency	34 North Brentwood St., Suite 14	St. Louis	MO	63105	314-727-7007

MISSISSIPPI

Color Campus Modeling School	2503 Meadow Dr., c/o Cala Campus	Biloxi	MS	39535	601-388-2465
Naomi's Modeling School	P.O. Box 8618	Columbus	MS	39705	601-328-3789

MONTANA

Creative World	3839 Dover Rd.	Billings	MT	59102	406-259-9540
Montana Mystique Talent Agency	P.O. Box 3244	Bozeman	MT	59772	406-586-6099

NORTH CAROLINA

Carolina Talent	227 West Trade St., Suite 2330	Charlotte	NC	28202	704-332-3218
Jan Thompson Agency	820 East Blvd.	Charlotte	NC	28203	704-377-5987
John Casablancas Center	830 Tyvola St., Suite 100	Charlotte	NC	28217-3537	704-523-6966
JTA Talent	820 East Blvd.	Charlotte	NC	28203	704-377-5987
Rory W. Medrano Modeling & Talent	1719-3 Euclid Ave.	Charlotte	NC	28203	704-376-0491
Cities Classic	859 Cloverleaf Plaza	Concord	NC	28025	800-860-5261
Charlotte Blume School	2523 Mirror Lake Dr.	Fayetteville	NC	28303	919-484-3466
Touch of Gold Modeling School	1304 East Mulberry St.	Goldsboro	NC	27530	919-736-4888
Brockman Associates Model Agency	P.O. Box 9502	Greensboro	NC	27408	919-288-3425
Directions USA	3717D Market St.	Greensboro	NC	27401	919-292-2800

Glamour	1600 E. Wendover Ave.	Greensboro	NC	27405	919-379-9039
Marilyn's Model Agency	601 Norwalk St.	Greensboro	NC	27407	919-292-5950
Metropolis Model & Talent	620 S. Elm St., Suite 330	Greensboro	NC	27406	919-691-1705
Talent Connection	338 N. Elm St., Suite 211	Greensboro	NC	27401	919-274-2499
Initial Impressions	P.O. Box 1026	Hickory	NC	28601	919-327-3349
Mar-Lyn Agency & School	716 4th St. S.W.	Hickory	NC	28601	919-322-9301
Joan Baker Studio	403 Country Club Acres	Kings Mtn	NC	28086	704-739-6868
D&S Talent	P.O. Box 3035, 101 South Main Street	Monroe	NC	28110	704-283-1659
Barbizon of Raleigh	4109 Old Wake Forest Rd.	Raleigh	NC	27609	919-876-8201
Raleigh Wood Casting & Talent	117 S.W. St.	Raleigh	NC	27603	919-829-3637
Delia Model Management	2422 Wrightsville Ave.	Wilmington	NC	28403	919-343-1753
Showpeople	P.O. Box 4458	Wilmington	NC	28406	919-313-0083
Touch of Class	805 S Tarboro St.	Wilson	NC	27893	919-291-6888
Capri & Associates	895 Peters Crk Pkwy., Suite 204	Winston-Salem	NC	27103	919-725-4102
Dancer & Company	1068 W. 4th St.	Winston-Salem	NC	27101	919-725-3281
U'Re Special Modeling & Charm School	1829 Butler St.	Winston-Salem	NC	27101	919-788-9566

NORTH DAKOTA

Academie Model-Talent Agency	220-1/4 Broadway	Fargo	ND	58102	701-235-8132
Cheri Paul Studio	W. Acres Shopping Center	Fargo	ND	58103	701-282-2268

NEBRASKA

Richard Lutz International	5625 "O"	Lincoln	NE	68510	402-483-2241
International School of Modeling	8602 Cass St.	Omaha	NE	68114	402-399-8787
Nancy Bounds International	4803 Davenport	Omaha	NE	68132	402-558-9292
Talent Pool	9136 Mormon Bridge Rd.	Omaha	NE	68506	402-476-0779
John Casablancas Center	661 North 50th	Omaha	NE	68132	402-558-6050
Dory Passolt Models	2030 North 72nd St.	Omaha	NE	68134	402-391-6831

NEW HAMPSHIRE

Vogue Modeling Agency	200 Bedford St.	Manchester	NH	03101	603-622-5661
New England Models Group	76 Northeastern Blvd., Suite 36	Nashua	NH	03062	603-595-7117
Cinderella Modeling Studio & Agency	9 Brook St.	Manchester	NH	03104	603-627-4125
Webb Model Management	1 Middle St.	Portsmouth	NH	03801	603-430-9334

NEW JERSEY

New Talent Management	590 Route 70, Suite 1C	Bricktown	NJ	08723	908-477-3355
Kathy Donahue's Model & Talent Agency	383 North Kings Hwy	Cherry Hill	NJ	08034	609-482-9113

Models on the Move	P.O. Box 4037	Cherry Hill	NJ	08034	609-428-7667
Zur Photographers	329 Myrtle St., P.O. Box 102	Cliffwood	NJ	07721	908-566-9282
Kookai	1 Bridge Plaza, Suite 400	Ft Lee	NJ	07024	201-592-5151
Harpers Models & Talent	42 Harmon Place N.	Haledon	NJ	07508	201-744-8877
Barbizon School of Highland Park	300 Raritan Ave.	Highland Pk	NJ	08904	908-846-3800
Deanna Trust Models	2 Green Village Rd.	Madison	NJ	07940	201-377-1788
Anderson Models	Route 73 N822, Suite A	Marlton	NJ	08053	609-596-7200
Barbizon of Mercerville	P.O. Box 2691 Hampton	Mercerville	NJ	08690	609-586-3310
Cleri Model Management	402 Main St., Suite 300	Metuchen	NJ	08840	908-632-9544
Barbizon School & Agency	70 Park St.	Montclair	NJ	07042	201-783-4030
Camelot Modeling Consultant	26 Park St.	Montclair	NJ	07042	201-509-8522
Harpers Model & Talent	484 Bloomfield Ave., Suite 5	Montclair	NJ	07042	201-744-8877
Meadowlands Modeling	7601 Broadway	North Bergen	NJ	07047	201-861-1106
Jonte Agency	42 Harmon Place	North Haledon	NJ	07508	201-423-5159
Sandi Stewart Talent Management	24 Plymouth Rd.	Nutley	NJ	07110	201-661-0350
Model Team Professional Studios	55 Central Ave.	Ocean Grove	NJ	07756	908-988-3648
Barbizon of Paramus	210 State Rte 4, Suite 210	Paramus	NJ	07652	201-909-0600
Talent Showcases	502 Madison Ave.	Paterson	NJ	07514	201-790-4030
G&O Models	103 W. Main St.	Rahway	NJ	07065	908-388-5537
Barbizon School	80 Broad St.	Red Bank	NJ	07701	908-842-6161
Delaware Valley Finishing	156 E 3rd Ave.	Runnameade	NJ	08078	609-939-4600
Dell Management Modeling Center	312 Ganttown Rd.	Sewell	NJ	08080	609-589-4099
Clancy Roz Casting	76 Wilfred Ave.	Titusville	NJ	08560	609-737-6955
Meredith Model Management	10 Furler St.	Totowa	NJ	07512	201-812-0122
Barbizon of Trenton	P.O. Box 2691, Hamilton Sq.	Trenton	NJ	08690	609-586-3310
West Model & Talent	1996 Morris Ave.	Union	NJ	07083	908-789-7463
Blanche Zeller Agency	28 Chestnut Rd.	Verona	NJ	07044	201-239-0202
Show Biz Kids	4015 Main St.	Voorhees	NJ	08043	609-424-7827
Christine Models & Casting	19 Castles Dr.	Wayne	NJ	07470	201-696-6950

NEW MEXICO

Eaton Germack Agency	3636 High St. N.E.	Albuquerque	NM	87107	505-344-3149
Flair Modeling & Talent Agency	7001 Menaul Blvd. N.E.	Albuquerque	NM	87110	505-881-4688
John Robert Powers	2021 San Mateo N.E., Suite J	Albuquerque	NM	87110	505-266-5677
Phoenix Agency	6400 Uptown Blvd N.E., Suite 481W	Albuquerque	NM	87110	505-881-1209
Southwest Models	12 County Rd. 3775	Farmington	NM	87499	505-327-0869

Mannequin Agency	2021 San Mateo N.E.	Albuquerque	NM	87110	505-266-6829
Aesthetics	489 Camino Don Miguel	Santa Fe	NM	87501	505-982-5883

NEVADA

Supreme Agency	4180 S. Sandhill Rd., Suite B8	Las Vegas	NV	89121	702-898-5627
Bass Creative Bookings	417 Bridger Ave.	Las Vegas	NV	89101	702-388-2898
Bobby Morris Agency	1629 E. Sahara Ave.	Las Vegas	NV	89104	702-733-7575
Charm Unlimited	880 E. Sahara Ave., Suite 106	Las Vegas	NV	89104	702-735-2335
Classic Models & Talent	3305 Spring Mountain Rd., Suite 12	Las Vegas	NV	89102	702-367-1444
Holidays Models	1909 Weldon Place	Las Vegas	NV	89109	702-735-7353
Las Vegas Models	3625 S. Mojave, Suite 8	Las Vegas	NV	89121	702-737-1800
Lenz Agency	1591 E. Desert Inn	Las Vegas	NV	89109	702-733-6888
Taylor Artist Management	4410 Skyview Dr.	Las Vegas	NV	89119	702-736-9450
Barbizon of Reno	4600 Kietzke Lane Bldg., Suite A104	Reno	NV	89502	702-825-4644

NEW YORK

Barbizon of Albany	1980 Central Ave.	Albany	NY	12205	518-456-6713
Barbizon of Babylon	8 Little East Neck Rd.	Babylon	NY	11702	516-587-6100
Design Model Agency	1919 RR 110	E. Farmingdale	NY	11735	516-293-7071
Working Models	70-10 Austin St.	Forest Hills	NY	11375	718-261-8780
Christina Models	55 S. Bergen Place, Suite 4E	Freeport	NY	11520	516-868-5932
Margo George Modeling Center	159 W. Main St., P.O. Box 176	Goshen	NY	10924	914-294-8144
Jennifer Models	501 Park Ave.	Huntington	NY	11743	516-385-4924
Barbizon of Syracuse	117 Metropolitan Park Dr.	Liverpool	NY	13088	315-457-7580
Barbara Thomas Agency	469 Albany-Shaker Rd.	Loudon	NY	12211	518-458-7849
Elaine Gordon Model Management	1926 Helen Ct.	Merrick	NY	11566	516-623-7736
Helene Models	200 North Ave., Floor 2, Suite 3	New Rochelle	NY	10801	800-606-7160
Focus International	62 Mont Peliere Circle	Rochester	NY	14618	716-461-1232
US Model & Talent Management	250 North Goodman St., Studio 36	Rochester	NY	14607	716-244-0592
Louise Boyka Studio	432 State St.	Schenectady	NY	12305	518-877-6681
Personal Best	3960 Harlem Rd.	Snyder	NY	14226	716-839-9012
All Talent Management	34 Clinton Ave.	Staten Island	NY	10301	718-447-4616
Joanne's Fashion & Charm Models	2201 Pinnacle Dr.	Utica	NY	13501	315-797-6424
National Talent Associates	40 Railroad Ave.	Valley Stream	NY	11580	516-825-8707
Barbizon of White Plains	190 East Post Rd	White Plains	NY	10601	914-428-2030
Gallian Media Images	202 Westchester Ave.	White Plains	NY	10601	914-948-4460
Wright Modeling	5225 Sheridan Dr.	Williamsville	NY	14221	716-632-4391

Wilhelmina Models	300 Park Ave. South	New York City	NY	10010	212-473-0700
Ford Modeling Agency	344 E. 59th St.	New York City	NY	10022	212-753-6500
Gap Models	301 W. 57th St.	New York City	NY	10019	212-586-2448
Plus Models Mgmt	49 W. 37th St.	New York City	NY	10018	212-997-1785
Gilla Roos	16 W. 22nd St.	New York City	NY	10010	212-727-7820
Rascals Unltd Agency	27 E. 77th St.	New York City	NY	10162	212-675-7314
Abrams Artists Assocs.	420 Madison Ave.	New York City	NY	10017	212-935-8980
Agents For The Arts	203 W. 23rd St.	New York City	NY	10011	212-229-2562
Michael Amato Agency	1650 Broadway	New York City	NY	10019	212-247-4456
American Int'l Talent Agency	303 W. 42nd St.	New York City	NY	10036	212-245-8888
Andreadis Talent Agency	119 W. 57th St.	New York City	NY	10019	212-315-0303
J Michael Bloom & Assocs.	233 Park Ave. South	New York City	NY	10003	212-529-6500
Bookers	150 Fifth Ave.	New York City	NY	10011	212-645-9706
Carson-Adler Agency	250 W. 57th St.	New York City	NY	10107	212-307-1882
4 B Talents	630 Ninth Ave.	New York City	NY	10036	212-268-2160
Dorothy Palmer Talent Agency	235 W. 56th St.	New York City	NY	10019	212-765-4280
Talent Plus	23 W. 68th St.	New York City	NY	10023	212-966-0064
Formation	156 Fifth Ave.	New York City	NY	10010	212-675-7037
Funnyface	151 E. 31st St.	New York City	NY	10016	212-686-4343
Marje Fields	165 W. 46th St.	New York City	NY	10036	212-764-5740

OHIO

Barbizon of Akron	3378 W. Market St.	Akron	OH	44333	216-867-4110
Pro Model Management	3378 W. Market St.	Akron	OH	44313	216-867-4125
Protocol Models	1969 N. Cleveland Massillon Rd.	Akron	OH	44333-1275	216-666-6066
Le Model	7536 Market St.	Boardman	OH	44512	216-758-4417
Michael Paul Agency	4165 15th St. N.W.	Canton	OH	44703	216-453-7120
Bette Massie Agency	415 St. Route 725, Normandy Square	Centerville	OH	45459	513-435-3477
Jack Moran Talent	5714 Scarborough Dr.	Cincinatti	OH	45238	513-451-8350
John Cassablancas Center	10680 McSwain Dr.	Cincinatti	OH	45241	513-733-8998
Ashley Talent Agency	128 E. Sixth St.	Cincinatti	OH	45202	513-381-6996
Barbara Proffitt Casting Agency	3563 Columbia Pkwy.	Cincinatti	OH	45226	513-533-1144
Cam Talent	1150 W. 8th St., Suite 262	Cincinatti	OH	45203	513-421-1795
Casablancas MTM	10680 McSwain Dr.	Cincinatti	OH	45241	513-733-8998
Cincinnati Model Agency	6047 Montgomery Rd.	Cincinatti	OH	45213	513-351-2700
Creative Talent	700 W. Pete Rose Way	Cincinatti	OH	45203	513-241-7827

Kathleen Wellman Modeling School	128 E. 6th St.	Cincinatti	OH	45202	513-381-6996
Urbane Acadamy	22 W. 7th St.	Cincinatti	OH	45202	513-381-7371
David & Lee Model	1127 Euclid Ave.	Cleveland	OH	44115	216-522-1300
Taxi Model Management	2044 Euclid Ave., Penthouse	Cleveland	OH	44115	216-781-8294
Cline & Mosic Talent Agency	369 W. 3rd Ave., Suite 202	Columbus	OH	43201	614-297-1711
Jeanette Grider School	1453 E. Main St.	Columbus	OH	43205	614-258-6787
John Casablancas Center	6322 Busch Blvd.	Columbus	OH	43229	614-847-0010
John M Moore Entertainment Company	P.O. Box 21466	Columbus	OH	43221	614-442-3949
John Robert Powers	5900 Roche St.	Columbus	OH	43229	614-846-1046
Noni Agency	172 E. State St., Suite 502	Columbus	OH	43215	614-224-7217
Sugar & Spice Model Agency	3558 Rand Court C	Columbus	OH	43227	614-238-0228
Sharkey Career School	1299-H Lyons Rd.	Dayton	OH	45458	513-434-4461
John Robert Powers	50 Baker Blvd.	Fairlawn	OH	44313	216-836-8422
Hogue Fox Models & Talent	5293 Dogwood Trail	Lyndhurst	OH	44124	216-449-0400
Sherry Lee Finishing School	7745 Cricket Circle N.W.	Massillion	OH	44646	216-833-2973
Tommy's New Attitude	3713 Lee Road	Shaker Heights	OH	44120	216-751-2006
Ron Lee International Agency	20496 Drake	Strongsville	OH	44136	216-238-3363
John Casablancas Model & Talent Management	1346 Secor Road, Suite 201	Toledo	OH	43623	419-474-2883
Margret O'Brien School	330 S. Reynolds Rd.	Toledo	OH	43606	419-536-5522
Traque Model Mamagement	708 W. Brancrott, Suite 2	Toledo	OH	43620	419-244-7363
The Right Direction	6660 North High St., Suite 3J	Worthington	OH	43085	614-848-3357

OKLAHOMA

Park Ave Modeling	515 N. Canadian Terr.	Mustang	OK	73064-6131	405-745-4982
A- Mazin	6051 N. Brookline., Suite 137	Oklahoma City	OK	73112	405-843-5583
Applause Studios	5800 S. Western	Oklahoma City	OK	73109	405-634-4792
Jo Ann Fullerton Modeling & Casting	1432 W. Britton Rd., Suite 201	Oklahoma City	OK	73114	405-848-4839
John Casablancas MTM	6520 NorthWestern Ave.	Oklahoma City	OK	73116	405-842-0000
OK Talent & Models	P.O. Box 25593	Oklahoma City	OK	73125	405-732-2212
Linda Layman Agency	3546 E. 51st St.	Tulsa	OK	74135	918-744-0888
Production Associates	5530 S. 79th East Place	Tulsa	OK	74145	918-622-2593
Sherack Studio	1727 S. Cheyenne Ave.	Tulsa	OK	74119	918-622-7038

OREGON

Barbizon	1140 Williagillespie Rd., Suite 15	Eugene	OR	97401	503-343-8666
Christiev Carothers Agency	1600 N. Riverside, Suite 1062	Medford	OR	97501	503-722-5452

ABC Kids, Performing Arts Center	3829 N.E. Tillamook	Portland	OR	97212	503-249-2945
Academy One	1510 S.W. 6th	Portland	OR	97210	503-227-4757
Pro Model	921 S.W. Morrison, Suite 506	Portland	OR	97205	503-228-5648
Talent Management NW	935 N.W. 19th Ave.	Portland	OR	97209	503-223-1931
Cinderella Models School & Agency	317 Court N.E.	Salem	OR	97301	503-581-1073
Cusick's Talent Agency	733 N.W. Everett	Portland	OR	97209	503-274-8555
John Robert Powers	2105 N.E. 28th Ave.	Portland	OR	97212	503-284-6274
Rose City Talent	123 N.E. 3rd Ave.	Portland	OR	97232	503-230-1255

PENNSYLVANIA

Image Elite	4959 Hamilton Blvd.	Allentown	PA	18106	215-391-9133
Jan Nagy School & Agency	226 North 7th St.	Allentown	PA	18102	215-820-5359
Barbizon School of Altoona	1130 13th Ave., Suite 1	Altoona	PA	16601	814-994-5016
Barbizon of Philadelphia	18 Greenfield Ave.	Ardmore	PA	19003	215-668-2080
Hot Foot, Lis Braun Agency	73 Academy Rd.	Bala Cynwyd	PA	19004	215-664-0674
Linda Johnston's Studio	3 Clyde Ln.	Broomall	PA	19073	215-356-3793
Marilyn E Kane Model School Management	1022 N. Main St.	Butler	PA	16001	412-287-0576
Perfections Modeling School & Agency	3117 Chestnut, Suite 201	Camphill	PA	17011	717-730-0985
Modeling Resource	37 S. Clinton St.	Doylestown	PA	18901	215-340-0900
Modeling & Promos by Riana	2617 Peach St., Suite 101	Erie	PA	16508	814-835-3930
Barbizon School & Agency	P.O. Box 5445	Harrisburg	PA	17110	717-234-3277
Donatelli Model Management	156 Madison Ave.	Hyde Park	PA	19605	215-921-0777
Main Line Models	160 King of Prussia Plaza	King of Prussia	PA	19406	215-337-2689
Plaza 7 Model & Talent Representatives	160 King of Prussia Plaza	King of Prussia	PA	19406	215-337-2689
Bowman Agency	P.O. Box 4071	Lancaster	PA	17604	717-898-7716
John Casablancas Center	920 Town Ctr Dr., Suite I-20	Langhorne	PA	19047	215-752-8600
Greer Lange Association	18 Great Valley Pkwy, Suite 180	Malvern	PA	19355	215-647-5515
Van Ents Model & Theatrical Agency	Sheraton Inn - Pittsburgh N., 910 Sheraton Dr. S.	Mars	PA	10646	412-776-3354
Folio Model	One Monroeville Center	Monroeville	PA	15146	412-372-8980
John Casablancas Center Model & Talent Agency	2735 Mosside Blvd., Suite 300	Monroeville	PA	15146	412-372-7373
John Casablancas Center	170 W. Germantown Pike, Suite C-3	Morristown	PA	19401	215-275-8843
JOY Academy of Modeling	580 Union Schl Rd.	Mt Joy	PA	17552	717-653-2133
Sierra Modeling & Talent	4 Terry Drive, Suite 17A	Newtown	PA	18940	215-579-2100
Queen of Prussia Charm School	3024 Pot Shop Road	Norristown	PA	19403	215-278-0780
Askins Models	New Market, Ste. 200, Headhouse	Philadelphia	PA	19147	215-925-7795

Expressions Agency	104 Church St.	Philadelphia	PA	19106	215-923-4420
Jim Carroll Models-Talent & Casting	7443 New 2nd St.	Philadelphia	PA	19126	
John Robert Powers	1528 Spruce St.	Philadelphia	PA	19102	215-732-4060
Life Workshop	225 Church St., Suite 1-I	Philadelphia	PA	19106	215-592-8400
Reinhard Model & Talent Agency	2021 Arch St., Suite 400	Philadelphia	PA	19103	215-567-2008
Ruth Harper School	1427 W. Erie Ave.	Philadelphia	PA	19140	215-225-4268
Barbizon School	9 Pkwy Court, 875 Greentree Rd, Suite 1	Pittsburgh	PA	15220	412-937-0700
Doherty Casting	109 Market St.	Pittsburgh	PA	15222	412-765-1400
Donna Belajac	One Bigelow Square, Suite 1924	Pittsburgh	PA	15219	412-391-1005
Mary Leister Charm & Finishing School	539 Court St.	Reading	PA	19601	215-373-6150
Highlite Modeling & Casting	415 N. 8th Ave.	Scranton	PA	18503	717-346-3166
Karisma Modeling & Promotions	301 Oxford Valley Rd., Suite 103B	Tsrdley	PA	19067	215-321-7660
Barbizon School	77 E. Market	Wilkes-Barre	PA	18702	717-823-3743

RHODE ISLAND

MTM Model Management	1383 Oaklawn Ave., Suite 12	Cranston	RI	02920	401-942-3422
Model Club	247 South Main St.	Providence	RI	02903	401-273-7120
John Cassablancas	1 Lambert Landing	Warwick	RI	02886	401-463-5866
Rhode Island Model Agency	725 West Shore Rd.	Warwick	RI	02889	401-739-2151

SOUTH CAROLINA

Fortress Model Management	1813 Wilkenson St.	Casey	SC	29033	803-739-2421
Kross Talent	2178 A Savannah Hwy.	Charleston	SC	29407	803-763-6385
Millie Lewis Model & Talent	1901 Ashley River Rd., Suite 6A	Charleston	SC	29407	803-571-7781
Carolina Winds Productions	119 Gadsen St.	Chester	SC	29706	803-581-2278
Collins Models Studio/Agency	1441 Greenhill Rd.	Columbia	SC	29206	803-782-5223
Jenny Trussell Modeling School	1030 Saint Andrew Rd.	Columbia	SC	29210	803-798-0553
LaBonze	117 Charles Wood Dr.	Columbia	SC	29206	803-699-7753
Lancelot Studios	1945 Decker Blvd., Suite 10	Columbia	SC	29606	803-787-5636
Millie Lewis of Columbia	#10 Calendar Ct., Suite A	Columbia	SC	29206	803-782-7338
Revelations	3021-6 McNaughton Rd.	Columbia	SC	29223	803-736-4586
The Proper Miss/Talent One	5516 Lakeshore Dr., Suite 410	Columbia	SC	29206	803-782-1060
Millie Lewis Agency of Greenville	1228 S. Pleasantburg Dr.	Greenville	SC	29605	803-299-1101
Showpeople Models & Talent	2103 Farlow St., Suite 110	Myrtle Beach	SC	29578	803-448-6684
Sterling Modeling	1349 Forest Brook Rd.	Myrtle Beach	SC	29557	803-236-1345
Barbizon of Charleston	2155A N. Park Lane	North Charleston	SC	29406	803-797-1417

Showcase Models	1200 33rd Ave. S.	North Myrtle Beach	SC	29582	803-272-8009
Betty Lane Models School & Agency	250 Doyle St.	Orangeburg	SC	29115	803-534-9472
The LH Fields Group	464 E Main St.	Spartenburg	SC	29302	803-579-0389

SOUTH DAKOTA

Bernice Johnson School & Agency	1320 South Minnesota Ave.	Sioux Falls	SD	57105-0654	605-338-3918
Haute Models. Inc	1002 West 6th St.	Sioux Falls	SD	57104	605-334-6110

TENNESSEE

Advantage Models & Talent	P.O. Box 3145	Brentwood	TN	37024	615-833-3005
Ambiance Modeling Agency	6925 Shallowford Rd., Suite 207	Chattanooga	TN	37421	615-499-1994
Daniels & Assocs.	732 Cherry St.	Chattanooga	TN	37402-1909	615-629-6216
Chaparral Talent Agency	P.O. Box 25	Ooltewa	TN	37363	615-238-9790
Barbizon of Memphis	6685 Poplar, Suite 202	Germantown	TN	38138	901-755-6800
Model World	155 Carriage House Dr.	Jackson	TN	38305	901-661-9551
18 Karat Talent & Modeling	8208 Rising Fawn Dr.	Knoxville	TN	37923	615-690-7240
Betty Rasnic Agency	2400 Merchants Dr.	Knoxville	TN	37912	615-525-7011
CJ's Training Center	406 11th St.	Knoxville	TN	37916	615-977-8735
Model Search	8905 Kingston Pike	Knoxville	TN	37923	615-453-1489
Premier Models, Talent & Training	408 Cedar Bluff Rd., Suite 363	Knoxville	TN	37923	615-694-7073
Premiere Model & Talent Agency	2400 Merchants Rd.	Knoxville	TN	37912	615-694-7073
Classique Image	P.O. Box 3036	Memphis	TN	38173	901-452-3356
Donna's School of Modeling	2988 Austin Pea Hwy.	Memphis	TN	38128	901-386-6654
Dot's Modeling	3126 Kimball Ave.	Memphis	TN	38114	901-276-6613
John Casablancas Center	6263 Poplar Ave., Suite 1052	Memphis	TN	38119	901-685-0066
John Robert Powers	5101 Sanderlin Ave., Suite 102	Memphis	TN	38117	901-682-9142
Robbins Model & Talent	1213 Park Place Mall, Suite 246	Memphis	TN	38119	901-761-0211
Taliesyn Agency	P.O. Box 1167	Memphis	TN	38111	901-523-0056
The Donna Groff Agency	P.O. Box 382517	Memphis	TN	382517	901-854-5561
AIM Model & Talent	Bellemeade Plz #205, 4544 Harding Rd.	Nashville	TN	37205	615-292-0246
Barbizon School & Agency	2000 Glen Echo Rd.	Nashville	TN	37217	615-298-4402
Flair Models	P.O. Box 17372	Nashville	TN	37217	615-361-3737
Harpers Agency	2400 Crestmore Rd., Suite 314	Nashville	TN	37215	615-383-1455
Jo-Susan Modeling School	2817 W. End Pl.	Nashville	TN	37203	615-327-8726

TEXAS

Malm Model Management	2446 Industrial Blvd.	Abilene	TX	79602	915-698-2673

Diane Dick Modeling Agency	2481 I-40 Hwy W.	Amarillo	TX	79109	806-353-9011
Susan's Modeling Agency & School	2201 S. W'ern St., Suite 121	Amarillo	TX	79109	806-352-1943
Creative Arts Theater & School CATS-	1100 W. Randol Mill Rd.	Arlington	TX	76012	817-274-6047
Actor's Clearing House	501 N. IH 35	Austin	TX	78702	512-476-3412
DB Talent	P.O. Box 3778	Austin	TX	78764	806-353-9011
Donna Adams Talent Agency	7739 Northcross Dr.	Austin	TX	78757	512-451-2278
K Hall Agency	101 West 6th St., Suite 518	Austin	TX	78701	512-476-7523
All Star Promos	P.O. Box 7519	Corpus Christi	TX	78415	512-852-3203
Fashion Showcase	5215 Embassy Dr.	Corpus Christi	TX	78411	512-855-5111
Infinity Modeling	4252-D S. Alameda, Suite C	Corpus Christi	TX	78412	512-993-4805
Reflections Fashion & Talent Agency	3817 S. Alameda, Suite C	Corpus Christi	TX	78411	512-857-5414
Barbara Walsh Agency	4501 Wildwood Rd.	Dallas	TX	75209	214-351-5920
Campbell Agency	3906 Lemmon Ave., Suite 200	Dallas	TX	75219	214-522-8991
Cherie Eaton	8720 Fawn Dr.	Dallas	TX	75238	214-644-5744
Clipse Model Management	3301 McKinney Ave., Suite 200	Dallas	TX	75204	214-720-0005
Dallas Model Group	12700 Hillcrest Rd., Suite 147	Dallas	TX	75230	214-980-7647
J&D Talent	1825 Market Ctr Blvd., Suite 320	Dallas	TX	75207	214-744-4411
John Robert Powers	13601 Preston Rd., Suite C-14	Dallas	TX	75240	214-239-9551
KD Studios	2600 Stemmons Frwy, Suite 117	Dallas	TX	75207	214-638-0484
Kim Dawson Agency	P.O. Box 585060, 1643 Apparel Mart	Dallas	TX	75258	214-638-2414
Mary Collins Agency	5956 Sherry Ln., Suite 506	Dallas	TX	75225	214-360-0900
Peggy Taylor Talent	1825 Mkt Ctr Blvd. #320A, Lock Box 37	Dallas	TX	75207	214-651-7884
Stars Over Texas	7021 John Carpenter Frwy	Dallas	TX	75247	214-638-6200
Talento Hispano	8204 Elmbrook Dr., Suite 117A	Dallas	TX	75247	214-638-5727
Tanya Blair Artist Management	4528 McKinney Ave., Suite 107	Dallas	TX	75205-3324	214-522-9750
Delat Studio	2719 N. Stanton	El Paso	TX	79902	915-544-0607
Forward Image Model Talent Management	1140 Airway Blvd., Suite 140	El Paso	TX	79902	915-778-1100
Fran Simon Model & Talent Agency	9611 Acer Ave.	El Paso	TX	79925	915-594-8772
John Casablancas Center	8900 Viscount Blvd. A-R	El Paso	TX	79925	915-598-9899
Talent House	604 Laurel	EL Paso	TX	79903	915-533-1945
Barbizon School	4950 Overtonridge	Ft Worth	TX	76132	817-294-0554
John Robert Powers	6320 Camp Bowie Blvd.	Ft Worth	TX	76116	817-738-2021
Talent Express	602 College, Suite 117A	Grand Prairie	TX	75050	
Actors & Models of Houston	7887 San Felipe, Suite 227	Houston	TX	77063	713-789-4973
Actors Etc.	2630 Fountain View, Suite 216	Houston	TX	77057	713-785-4495

APM Studio	5020 FM 1960 W., Suite A4	Houston	TX	77069	713-440-6509
Barbizon of Houston	5433 Westheimer Ave., Suite 300	Houston	TX	77056	713-8509111
First Models & Talent Agency	5433 Westheimer Ave., Suite 310	Houston	TX	77056	713-850-9611
Gary Chason Casting	908 Wood St.	Houston	TX	77002	713-227-8293
Inter-Media Model & Talent Agency	5353 W. Alabama, Suite 222	Houston	TX	77056	713-622-8282
Neal Hamil Agency	7887 San Felipe, Suite 227	Houston	TX	77063	713-789-1335
Pastorini-Bosby Talent Agency	3013 Fountain View, Suite 240	Houston	TX	77057-6120	713-266-4488
Sherry Young/Mad Hatter Talent Agency	6620 Harmin, Suite 270	Houston	TX	77036	713-266-5800
South Coast Studio	11200 Westheimer Blvd., 9th Floor	Houston	TX	77069	713-789-2787
Talent Place	5020 1960 West, Suite A-2	Houston	TX	77069	713-893-9191
Top Models Agency	Arena Tower Two, #1870, 7324 S.W. Freeway	Houston	TX	77074-2013	713-777-4949
Margo Manning Casting & Acting Studio	6221 N. O'Connor Rd., Suite 210	Irving	TX	75039	214-869-2323
Sherita Lynne Modeling Agency	320 Ruthlynn	Longview	TX	75608	903-758-1259
Robert Spence School/Agency	7200 Quaker Ave., Suite 53	Lubbock	TX	79424	806-797-8134
P.S. Images	1105 Pueblo Dr.	Midland	TX	79705	915-683-0844
Vicki Eisenberg Agency	929 Fernwood Dr.	Richardson	TX	75080	214-918-9593
Avant Models & Casting	8700 Crownhill Rd., Suite 503	San Antonio	TX	78209	210-308-8411
Condra & Co Talent Agency	13300 Old Blanco Rd., Suite 201	San Antonio	TX	78216-7739	210-492-9947
John Casablancas Center	3201 Cherry Ridge St., Suite 323	San Antonio	TX	78230	512-349-4185
Sinclair Modeling & Talent Agency	4115 Mediacal Dr., Suite 401	San Antonio	TX	78229	210-614-2281

UTAH

Finishing Touch	3725 Washington Blvd., Suite 5	Ogden	UT	84403	801-394-3771
Barbizon of Salt Lake	1363 S. State, Suite 232	Salt Lake City	UT	84115	801-487-7591
John Casablancas Center	2797 S. Main St., Suite A	Salt Lake City	UT	84115	801-484-2402
KLC Casting	772 W. South Temple	Salt Lake City	UT	84104	801-364-7447
Mc Carthy Agency	1326 Foothill Blvd.	Salt Lake City	UT	84108	801-581-9292
Executive Model Shop	9480 Union Sq., Suite 203	Sandy	UT	84070	813-755-1757
Burton & Perkins Agency	1326 South Soothill Blvd.	Salt Lake City	UT	84108	801-581-9292
Mary Pats Finishing School	270 Donlee Dr.	St George	UT	84770	801-634-9248

VIRGINIA

John Casablancas Center	249 S. Van Dorn	Alexandria	VA	22304	703-823-5200
Jackie Fenderson	1224 W. Roslyn Rd.	Colonial Heights	VA	23834	804-526-0609
Ann L School of Modeling	117 N. High St.	Harrisonburg	VA	22801	703-434-6664
Erickson Modeling Agency	1483 Chainbridge Rd., Suite 105	McClain	VA	22101	703-356-4251

New Faces Model Management	1861 Canon Blvd., Suite G	Newport News	VA	23606	804-873-1402
Write Modeling of VA	12638-16 Jeferson Ave.	Newportnews	VA	23602	804-886-5884
New York Modeling Agency	1225 Boissevain	Norfolk	VA	23507	804-626-3875
Talent Connection	809 Brandon Ave., Suite 5TE	Norfolk	VA	23501	804-624-1975
Ann Moody	Rt. 1 Box 666	Port Republic	VA	24471	703-289-5762
New Model	1982 Solaridge Ct.	Reston	VA	22091	703-620-9121
Cameo Models	7907 Fitzhugh, Suite 200	Richmond	VA	23221	804-355-1377
Richmond Modeling School	4914 Fitzhugh Ave., Suite 20	Richmond	VA	23230	804-359-1331
Cappa Chell Models	1950 Old Gallows Rd., Suite 500	Vienna	VA	22180	703-893-9500
New Faces Models	8230 Leesburg Pike	Vienna	VA	22180	703-821-0786
Glamour Agency	1115 Independence, Suite 110	Virginia Beach	VA	23455	804-363-8844
Charm Association Agency	144 Business Park Dr., Suite 100	Virginia Beach	VA	23462	804-490-8340
Sharon Agency	2345 Haversham Close	Virginia Beach	VA	23454	804-496-9666
Steinhart/Norton Agency	312 Arctic Cres	Virginia Beach	VA	23451	804-422-8535
Ward Agency	105 N. Plaza Trail	Virginia Beach	VA	23452	804-481-5930

VERMONT

The Pro Team at Promark Models	2 Church St.	Burlington	VT	05401	802-660-3717
Winning Ways	5 Maryland St.	S. Burlington	VT	05401	802-658-5750

WASHINGTON

ABC Kids	924 Bellevue Way N.E., Suite 200	Bellevue	WA	98004	206-646-5440
John Casablancas Center	155 108th Ave. N.E., Suite 600	Bellevue	WA	98004	206-646-3585
Kids Team	3431 96th Ave.	Bellevue	WA	98004	206-455-2969
Tri City Models	4415 W. Clearwater	Kennewick	WA	99336	509-783-5868
Troy Fair Modeling School & Agency	1522 Jay Way	Mt. Vernon	WA	98273	206-336-2960
Select Models	2307 S.E. 8th Dr.	Renton	WA	98055	206-682-5632
Actors Group	219 First Ave S.	Seattle	WA	98121	206-624-9465
Barbizon of Seattle	1501 4th Ave., Suite 305	Seattle	WA	98101	206-223-1500
Book Models	1700 Westlake Ave. N.	Seattle	WA	98109	206-286-8888
Carol James Talent Agency	117 S. Main St.	Seattle	WA	91804	206-447-9191
Eileen Seals International Model Agency	600 Stewart St., Plaza 600 Building	Seattle	WA	98101	206-448-2040
Lola Hallowell Agency	1700 Westlake Ave. N., Suite 436	Seattle	WA	98109	206-281-4646
Seattle Models Guild	1809 7th Ave.	Seattle	WA	98101	206-622-1406
TCM Modeling School & Agency	2200 6th Ave., Suite 100	Seattle	WA	98121	206-728-4826
Team Models	3431 96th Ave.	Seattle	WA	98101	206-455-2969
Drezden School	N 707 Division	Spokane	WA	99202	509-326-6800

PJ & Co Models International	9612 E. Sprague	Spokane	WA	99206	509-922-8102
Andersen Models International	3030 68th Ave. W., Suite G	Tacoma	WA	98466	206-564-5830
Blast Model &Talent Agency	11700 N.E. 95th St., Suite 120	Vancouver	WA	98682	206-892-0015
Professional School of Modeling	18 N. 59th Ave.	Yakima	WA	98908	509-965-1151

WISCONSIN

A Wilson Modeling	103 E. College, Suite 302	Appleton	WI	54911	414-738-7222
A&M Talent Casting	3110 W. Spencer St.	Appleton	WI	54912	414-731-6088
Model Workshop	4321 N. College Ave.	Appleton	WI	54914	414-733-1212
First Choice	1838 Greenfield Ave.	Green Bay	WI	54313	414-865-7916
Gered Models International	2702 Monroe St.	Madison	WI	53711	608-238-6372
Arlene Wilson Talent	809 S. 60th St.	Milwaukee	WI	53214	414-778-3838
Jennifer's Talent	740 N. Plankinton Ave., Suite 300	Milwaukee	WI	53203	414-277-9440
John Robert Powers	700 N. Water St.	Milwaukee	WI	53202	414-273-4468
Lori Lins	1301 N. Astor St.	Milwaukee	WI	53202	414-271-2288

WEST VIRGINIA

World of Models	951 Lake View Drive	Parkersburg	WV	26101	304-422-6131

Index

Pictures, 40-45, 59, 82-83, 85, 119
Portfolio, 85, 131
Print work, 92, 110-111
Producer, 26, 117

Reading skills, 95
Rejection, 25-26
Residuals, 95-96, 131
Resume, 131
Role-playing, 22-23, 95-96
"Ross Report," 36

Scams, 67-71
Schools and pageants, 87-89
Sears, 64
Set, 132
Shoot, 132
Shyness, 18-19, 88
Size, 21, 23-24, 28, 93
Stage parent, definition of, 132
Summer kids and other
    opportunities, 47-50

Talent manager, 117-119
Talent scout, 43
Taxes, 103
Tearsheets, 85, 132
Teeth, 24, 124
Television commercials, 95-97
Test photographer, definition of, 132
Test shot, definition of, 132

UltimateSource on-line casting
    service, 43

Vogue magazine, 115, 124
Voucher, 102, 132

Wardrobe, 83-85, 89, 124-126, 132
Work permit, 102

Zitner, Marilyn, 117-119

More information about the world of child modeling... just pick up your phone!

Child Modeling Quarterly ~ newsletter
Essential reference guide for parents who want to learn about the ins and outs of the modeling industry. Updated information throughout the year. 1 year subscription (4 issues) $14.95 Item #: 002.

"Getting Your Kids Into Commercials" ~ video
Discover the secrets of getting your kids started in television. Interviews with industry insiders, agents, producers and directors give you and your children the knowledge and experience they have acquired through years of experience in the business. If you have wondered if your child is the right type for TV commercials, this tape will give you the ability to make an accurate appraisal. $14.95 Item #: 003.

Wilhelmina Models T~shirt
Show off your model good looks with an Official Wilhelmina Models T-shirt. The 100% cotton white T-shirt has the Wilhelmina Models logo in black and red on the front and back. Adult sizes M, L, XL. $19.95. Item #: 005. Child T-shirts available in sizes S (6-8), M (10-12). $14.95 Item #: 010.

To order please call
1-800-889-MODEL

Kid Search
Annual nationwide model contest for kids ages newborn to 17 years. Prizes include Wilhelmina Models contracts and college scholarships. No experience necessary. Past winners have gone on to do advertising for companies including Playskool, Macy's, Hasbro, Guess?, and *Seventeen* Magazine.

To receive an entry form call
1-800-543-7663